I am closing that door

LORNE DRISCOLL

Copyright © 2015

The moral right of Lorne Driscoll to be identified as the author has been asserted by her in accordance with the Copyright, Designs and Patents Act 1988. All rights reserved. No part of this book may be used or reproduced, stored in a retrieval system, or transmitted in any form, or by any means electronic, mechanical, recording, photocopying, or in any manner whatsoever without permission in writing from the author, except for the inclusion of brief quotations in a review.

National Library of Australia Cataloguing-in-Publication entry

Creator: Driscoll, Lorne Sheree, author.
Title: I am closing that door / Lorne Sheree Driscoll.
ISBN: 9780994201508 (paperback)
ISBN: 9780994201515 (ebook)
Subjects: Driscoll, Lorne Sheree,Adult child sexual abuse victims–Biography. Sexual abuse victims' writings.Spiritual healing–Biography.
Dewey Number: 362.76092

Cover Page inspired by Damien Volkner
Book Cover Layout: Marion Duke- O'Callaghan (Pickawoowoo)
Publishing Consultants - Pickawoowoo Publishing Group

All rights reserved.

No part of the book may be transmitted or reproduced by any form or means, either mechanical or electronic, including recording and photocopying, or by any known storage and retrieval system, without the written consent of the author, except in the case of short quotations being used in a review

The views and opinions expressed in this work are solely those of the author and do not necessarily reflect the views of the publisher or publishing consultants, and they hereby disclaims any responsibility for them. No warranties or guarantees are expressed or implied by the publisher's choice to include any of the content in this volume.

This book is designed to provide information and motivation to readers and is not intended as a substitute for the medical advice of physicians, a professional mental health counsellor, or to provide professional psychological services to you. If you need expert professional assistance,

Contents of Book

Acknowledgments vii

Special Acknowledgment x

Foreword xi

Introduction xiv

The Brick Wall 1

The English Connection 4

Brainstorm... 8

Start of Counselling Notes...15

What I Am 33

Telling My Children..35

Feeling the Fear 49

Make a Goal 53

Letter to Relative 1 56

Pictures.. 69

you should seek the services of a competent mental health professional. Neither the publisher nor the individual author shall be responsible or liable for any person or entity with respect to any loss or damage caused, or alleged to have been caused, directly or indirectly, by the information contained in this book. The publisher nor author shall be responsible for physical, psychological, emotional, financial, or commercial damages, including, but not limited to, special, incidental, consequential or other damages. Our views and rights are the same: You are responsible for your own choices, actions, and results.

Reading this book can bring back strong unpleasant thoughts and feelings. These could even lead to thoughts of suicide or other injury. If you find yourself overwhelmed by these thoughts or feelings, please seek professional mental health services immediately!

Every effort has been made to make this book as accurate as possible. However, there may be mistakes, both typographical and in content. Furthermore, it may contain information that is not current practice. You are urged to learn as much as possible about child sexual abuse from all available sources and to tailor the information to your own individual needs.

Boat Trip 83

Silently Screaming.. 94

The Big Relative 2 Letter 102

Paedophile and Protégé 111

Last Visit... 123

Letter to Tokoroa Entity.................................126

Immeasurable Emotions.................................131

Work Secret..136

Letter to All 3 of Them 139

Letter to the Readers......................................142

The Impact of Writing This Book....................146

Appendix and Suggested Reading 160

I dedicate this book to all that have suffered abuse, to whatever extreme.

Acknowledgments

It has taken a very, very long time, for me to get to this point, and there are more than a few people in my journey who I would like to thank or acknowledge. As without them, I wouldn't be writing this book, of that I am sure.

Amongst those people are my son and daughter Damien and Jocelyn, they have been my saviours on many occasions. I am extremely proud of them both. They are my joy and jubilation in life. I love them deeply, with all my heart. I would like to thank them from the bottom of my heart and beyond, for allowing me to go through this process, My Way. I would also like to thank their respective partners as their understanding and compassion has been appreciated.

I would also like to thank my New Zealand Osteopath, Adrian Turner and my Counsellor, Helen Torr, who both helped in healing some of my past and counselled me through gaining an understanding, of why I went through, what I went through. Thank you both for your professional help, my time with both of you, was the beginning of

I am closing that door

this journey of pre-writing this book.

I would also like to thank my sister Leah, my little brother Blair and my dearest friend Katrina Briggs, who gave me the compassionate strength, blessing and encouragement to come forward and write this book. They even strengthened me, when the emotional strain of writing this book, was getting the better of me.

I have heartfelt thanks, to my son Damien Volkner, who surprised me and suggested that he had an idea for my cover page and did an illustration for my cover page. Consequently this illustration has become the inspiration for the cover. I love the fact that my son is accompanying me, from a distance, on this journey.

Big thanks to a friend and Proof Reader of my book, who wishes to remain unnamed. Thanks for letting me push the send button to you with my book as an attachment. Doing that has given me the stepping stone to passing this book onto the Publisher.

My deepest thanks to Inge Benda for her support in letting me breathe out my emotions that became exposed after putting pen to paper. She created a safe haven and allowed me to dissipate many emotions that were imbedded in me, as a young child. In turn allowing me to go ahead and send this to the Publisher.

My heartfelt thanks to Diego Franca, the Australian Osteopath I visited, he gave me the courage to put a timeline on this book, so I can let go off it. Fear was putting me of sending this to the actual Publisher. With both Inge's and Diego's help this is going to be an eventuality. This book needs to be out there, so it can help others.

There have been a few people through the course of my journey, who I won't name, for privacy reasons. I would like to thank them for sharing their own personal stories with me. The courage they took to open their hearts and let me know what they went through, was treasured. Only reconfirming, that I am not the only one, to have gone through what I went through. Thank you.

Thanks to Carla Van Raay who wrote God's Callgirl – A memoir and her subtle suggestions in the improvement of my manuscript.

Bless you all from the bottom of my heart.

Special Acknowledgment

A special acknowledgment goes to my dad, Jim Driscoll (1937–2002). His dream was to become a writer; unfortunately, he didn't get to pursue that dream. It now appears I am now living that dream of his. I would like to see his dream come true and at least, see his name in print within a book.

Once again, bless you all, from the bottom of my heart.

Foreword

There is a saying out there that says, there is always three sides to the story. Those three sides are my truth, your truth and the truth. This book is my side of the story, the truth of what I experienced, when growing up as a child. This truth is written from my personal perspective, as seen through my eyes, so therefore; in many places within the book, I say my truth, as it is my own truth and my own feelings. Everything I say within this book is the truth.

My book is letting you know, as the reader, how long it can actually take to heal from this type of trauma. That there is a process out there, of coming to terms from the shocking childhood that I went through. This is my personal process of what I went through, as I no longer wanted to be divined by my childhood. By writing and publishing this book, I am letting the reader know, parents especially, this can happen, if you are not watching or *listening* for the signs. The following are only a few of the signs I am talking about. When your little girl, who never throws tantrums, suddenly throws a wobbly and doesn't want to do, what you insists she does; especially when it involves something do with other family members or other adults that interact with the family. Another sign could be that your son (yes, this does happen to boys as well) suddenly develops a stutter, especially when under pressure and you wonder why! Your children or child begs and pleads with you not to go out and leave them alone with a babysitter or older siblings for instance. Or your child is suddenly retreating to her room, where as before she used to bring her toys to the lounge to play with. When your very own brother or other adult that is close to the family or interacts with the family a lot, is always asking to baby-sit your kids for you and might even keep manipulating you to go out, just so he can babysit your children; this is also another sign. If you feel like there is something wrong, then often there is. This trauma or abuse can happen from an extremely young age (could still be in the cradle age) and carry on to any age; whether male or female.

As a parent, I will also mention here that my book also lets the reader know, especially parents, that this is actually happening. This trauma happened under my parents' roof and my parents were not aware. I wonder how many more households out there, this is happening to and the parents/care-givers are not aware, whether it was in the past or in the now.

But upmost and most importantly, I am putting this information out there, because I hope it will help someone, just anyone, go through the healing process that they might need, no matter how immense or how minor that healing process might be. I can tell you, that writing this book has been my saving grace and I hope that it will be a saving grace for others out there. I am also suggesting that if you are going through this trauma, or have been through this trauma and haven't yet pursued help, that you go to your nearest helpline or confidante, whether that is a counsellor, professional helpline or even a personal confidante, where possible and as soon as possible.

P.S. Where I mentioned in this book, sending my book (manuscript) to the Publisher, I was advised by the initial publisher to embrace self publishing which had far less restrictions. After due reflection this is what I chose to do.

Introduction

I am writing this because I know this book will help lots of people out there. It will help them know, that they are not on their own. It will help them to know, that they are not the only one that is going through this, or have been through, what I went through. I am writing this book, as I hope to give someone out there the words, or some words to help them express what they are going through. I am writing this book, in the hope that it will be a healing process for someone out there. I am writing this, because for so long now I have, like too many other people out there, *kept silent* for way too long. There are many, many people out there that this has happened to, from one extreme to the other, either directly or indirectly. My purpose is not to make this book into a novel, but hopefully it will be more like a help book. My book is a really candid story of how it was in my childhood. No one persons' story is alike. A help book for all is not achievable from me, as I am not a professional, this is my personal story. So this will be like a help book to those who it suits, for others it will hopefully be the closest thing where viable, hence the use of my notes in this book, that can be referred to at any time.

I am about to bring what happened to me out in the open, for all to know. By writing this book, it will be giving my Inner Child the voice she needs. I know that this will be a healing process for me, my Inner Child, as well as for many others out there. This book is my truth, this is how I see it and I want others to see it, how I see it. I don't want to hold on to this any longer. *Silenced, but no longer,* I'm about to *brave the unknown* and tell it like it was.

My life, as a child was a horrifying life to go through. Life was unbearable. I didn't know that as a child though. At the time as a child, what I went through happened that often that it got to the stage that I thought it was normal. By the same token, even at such a young age, I knew that this shouldn't be happening. As an adult I never thought I would come through, what I went through and come out the other side, but I did. I am a hard working citizen with strong morals and I brought up 2 wonderful and lovely, independent children. I often wonder how I did that. I often think, with what I went through, as a child, it is amazing that I stayed sane enough to bring my children up. But I did and *I* did my best, within the circumstances that life presented to me, to make sure my energies, to the best of my abilities, were focused on making sure that my children didn't go through, what I went through.

As mentioned above, I think the best way I can tell my story is to include my notes from my counselling sessions. These

I am closing that door

notes will be typed, as they were hand written at the time and therefore, I will not be editing my counselling notes. I will type my notes as they were written in the moment, in their raw truth, they made sense and were needed at the time. I will fill in some gaps in black type, so they are more understandable to the reader. My notes will be typed in red type. I will share some of the pictures that I drew at the time, not that I am a fantastic drawer, far from it. But, it just might help someone out there, make sense of what they are going through or have been through. Maybe someone might even recognise it, as something that they themselves have done, just out of pure frustration and not understanding, why they are feeling, like they are feeling in the moment.

This book will be giving my Inner Child the voice she needs. However, the letters, which I wrote to the 3 people concerned, they alone would stand by themselves, to give my Inner Child the voice she needs.

Please note, relationship status, names and initials, for those concerned, within this book have been changed. Referring to the 3 people concerned above, I will refer to the 1st one as relative 1 and the 2nd as relative 2 or at times as big relative 2, where appropriate in text. The last one will remain as Tokoroa Entity; I don't need to change this one because I don't remember his actual name.

The Brick Wall

It came to the crunch for me early 2010 in New Zealand when, as they say 'you hit a brick wall'. My 'brick wall' at the time and yes, there has been heaps of 'brick walls' in my life, not just in the form of car accidents. The 'brick wall' that got me onto the path of writing this book, was not long after I had a car accident. This accident was an unforeseen side swipe to my car (the last of four car accidents that I have been through. Interestingly, all of which have been side swipes). That particular accident or brick wall put me in the path of an Osteopath.

His term at the time of the initial diagnoses was "Prolonged Whiplash…" Little did I know in that moment that he gave me that initial diagnoses, that he would eventually, put me onto the path of a Counsellor for rape victims. He put me in her direction, because memories of being abused as a young child came flooding back to me, during the time I was being treated for 'Prolonged Whiplash'.

His treatment and his bedside manner helped me feel comfortable enough to confide in him, when he did some

I am closing that door

work on my diaphragm. The diaphragm is where the body stores emotion, he told me. It was during one of those sessions that he was working on my diaphragm, that I felt I needed to say the words that were on my mind and eventually I did. I felt I needed to say the words, to release the words, therefore releasing the emotion. The words just came out in the end. I ended up telling my Osteopath, that I was raped as a young girl. I am now so glad, that I let those words go. So glad they came out, to be heard, for many reasons and in the moment, it was an emotional release. It was the first time I had ever said those words to someone within the Health Industry. I have no regrets, saying those words out loud. I have no regrets, those words were heard. I have no regrets that he linked me to my Counsellor and especially this particular Counsellor. It certainly seemed to go hand in hand with the treatment I had just received from my Osteopath.

It was my Counsellor's suggestion that I write my feelings/ thoughts down. Especially when I felt emotional or felt a trigger, that brought back memories from my childhood. So I could begin to recognize, those patterns that I had created from my childhood.

Her suggestion worked well. I found when I was writing what was on my mind, in the moment, getting off my mind by getting it on paper, sometimes allowed other thoughts and memories to come through. I found myself in tears many, many times. I also experienced many other emotions, some which were extremely turbulent and unsettling, while going through this process and period of writing. The writing of these notes was and still is as I am typing this book, a healing process, a letting go, if you like.

The English Connection

Before I carry on with typing the notes from my counselling session, I am going explain the English connection. This is another factor, which enticed me to write this book. Not that I am going to mention names but there were people, that I was coming in contact with, before and during the time, I started my journey of writing this book. These particular people were either English and/or connected to someone, that is English and they had the same or similar past as me. This to me meant a lot, a definite connection there for me, if you like. Not that I am distracting from the fact that I know abuse, whether sexual or otherwise, is a world-wide problem, far from it.

But England is my birth country. England is where being abused started for me (it didn't stop there, it continued when we got to New Zealand). Just like those English people, or their connection, I was coming into contact with, that is where their abuse happened. So I felt I needed to talk about England, as it brought that common ground together for me.

I am not about to go into the actual history of England. I just want to say, England has centuries and centuries of history. Since practically the beginning of time, there has been a history of keeping things 'hush, hush' and 'don't tell anyone' attitude, or being suppressed, or scared into '*keeping silent*', especially when it comes to abuse. Whether it's sexual or otherwise. Not just within the everyday community, but it is well known and well publicised that abuse has happened within religious communities/sects, as well. We all know that there has been a history of people being banished and/or even worse, killed for telling the truth.

Again, not that I am going to go into detail, but some of the stories and you could say some of those stories are barbaric from the English history, have horrified and disturbed me. Just like other countries histories, England is not on her own, with her barbaric history.

My point I am trying to make here is: I come from a country that has more or less been, dare I use the word, brainwashed, into hiding or 'sweeping under the carpet' some of those horrific happenings. Even in today's society, they will still 'sweep under the carpet' what is happening, because they have been doing it for centuries. England is not the only Country that does this.

That is one thing that I am not going to do, anymore. I

I am closing that door

am not going to 'sweep under the carpet' something so horrific, something that happened to me as a young child. No one deserves to go through what I went through, let alone a young child. In this case, I was not the only child in my family that went through the horrific childhood that I went through. I am going to help and break this cycle on a spiritual level, by putting this book out there.

I am now even going to say, even though I have no evidence, I am purely going on my gut instinct here. I believe that particular violator, who abused me in England, more than likely abused other family member(s) on his side, as well. The other family members I have in mind would generally, all be of similar age to us.

That believe came a little more evident for me, when for the first time, since leaving in 1972; I visited England in 2007. While I was in England, I visited my Nan in hospital who had been admitted, while I was in England. During that time I was there with her, in her hospital room, she had another visitor arrive. He was one of my violators and my relative 1.

Another relation was there at the time, with her family. After a while, that violator suggested that he take me home, where I was staying at the time. Before I had the chance to respond, she piped up and told him, "No, it's already planned, she is coming with us…" Even though it was already planned and even though I didn't need her to talk for me, I am glad she piped up and said, what she said.

As we left the hospital room the other relation, who was there with her family – who I hadn't seen, since leaving England in the first place (I did meet up with her a night or two, before this hospital visit), grabbed my hand and briskly walked us out of the hospital. I had that sense, even though it was left unsaid, that she was protecting me. I am not going to mention her name for privacy reasons, but I do thank her for that interaction and I thank her for meeting up with me when needed. It was great catching up with her.

Brainstorm

I have decided to put here a depiction of the Brainstorm I was playing with during the time I was considering writing this book. As limited as it is, I will include this here, as this might put some light, and/or understanding there for someone that has gone through, or is going through abuse. Or this Brainstorm might help others out there who have *not* gone through abuse, gain *some* understanding of someone who has been abused, or still is going through abuse.

What I have put in the Brainstorm is very limited, in the emotions and feelings, which from a personal point of view can be very intense, and/or 'mind-blowing'. The words to explain, what you might be experiencing or feeling, generally cannot be found or can be indescribable. Or some of those people affected, could have buried or blocked from their memories that this abuse has even happened to them, but will still experience unexplained turbulent emotional turmoil.

A lot of people who have gone through abuse, generally have no way of explaining how intense, turbulent and fragile their lives have been, and in a lot of cases still are. They find it very hard to explain what they might be thinking or feeling, when it comes to the abuse they either have suffered, or are suffering, whether sexual abuse or other abuse. That is probably one reason why it has taken me this long to get this far. I have finally got to the point where I can put words on paper. I can now pour my heart and soul out onto this laptop and put it out there, for all to read.

I have been through many healing processes in the past, even before I started my sessions with a rape counsellor. Now I am this far in my healing process, here I am putting it all in a book, which will be yet another healing process, not just for me, but for my Inner Child. I am hoping that by putting it out there, what I went through, might help someone else out there put at least some words to what they are feeling, and/or experiencing. I hope to give someone at least, some words to express their deepest and darkest feelings on this subject, which seems to be very taboo in, not just some societies but a lot of societies.

Please note, as this brainstorm was not readable as a picture, I have decided not to include the actual picture here. What I will do is list the middle subject as a heading and all the bubble thoughts from that heading I will list underneath. This list will be in red type just like my Counsel notes will be.

I am closing that door

Fearing The Unknown – Telling It Like it was:

Is this what love is? How do I know?

What 2 expect?

Not wanting 2 talk about it

How do I cope with this?

Disgraced, befriended my family, friends and other support people, supported me in this journey, but you can also be befriended by the perpetrator, which could be disguise of their intent, cheated, hurt

Friend + S.B. (Initials changed).

What do I say?

- How do I say it!!
- Versus.
- Not wanting to tell

How do I act?

Can I trust again? Trust became one of my biggest concerns. I had lost trust a long time ago. To learn to trust again, can be hard but it is also achievable.

How do I cope?

What could/will happen?

Shame and all the other emotions. This could be that you are feeling exposed and experience emotions that are turbulent, extreme emotions. Some of those emotions can be just, for instance, a sad emotion and you might not have any idea, why you are feeling this way.

B.U./prints. (Initials changed).

Life!!

Curling up in a ball

Saving the ones that hurt me

Wanting to give up CS 3x

The wanting to give up mentioned above, is just that. There were times when I did want to give up, when I was a lot younger than I am now. I wanted to end the continuous extreme emotional turmoil, I was going through. I now realise at the time, I was feeling all the emotions and punishing grief that I felt during my childhood. The human mind is a mysterious and wonderful thing but at times it can play havoc. I had buried what happened to me so well. Unbeknown to me, in those moments there was, deep inside of me an unrecognized abused, wounded and terrified child, which needed to be heard. She needed to come to terms with what happened to her. If I was having a problem, coping with all that extreme turmoil as an adult, imagine what a young child must be going through. How does a young child, handle all that extreme turmoil?

I can sort of answer that, from a personal perspective. They try to handle it by blocking out the hurt, suffering and trauma they are going through. They try to handle it by fantasising, or pretending that this is not actually happening to them. They try to handle it by escaping into their own world when they can, or play with a favourite toy or the likes, just so they can be by themselves, just so they can be alone. I am positive that my spirit must have disappeared somewhere at times, when this was happening to me, all as a survival mechanism.

However, I am not a professional and cannot answer the extremities of the psychological damage that a young child or even an adult would go through. What I do know is, apart from what I have read and seen through the media and witnessed and/or heard from others that I know. I went through my own psychological issues, in coping with something that was so traumatic and horrifying. Other people go through their own issues, whether it is from one extreme or the other extreme.

During this period of my life, when I did want to give up, I thought there was no way to stop the punishing turmoil I was experiencing, as it was exceptionally intense, mind blowing and having that feeling of having no control. I was feeling extremely powerless and alone, at times. The not understanding why I was going through this as well, as I had blocked so much from my memory. I eventually broke down, more than several times and eventually burnt out, more than once. It didn't help that at the time as well; I was also going through a tremendously stressful relationship with my husband and I realise now, he was tapping into my past emotional grief. He was tapping into the psychological trauma of the unrecognized abused, wounded and terrified child within me. I remember three times, during that period of extreme turmoil, I contemplated and went through the *beginnings* of the process, of trying to commit suicide. Just wanting to eliminate the risky, turbulent turmoil I was experiencing, as it was more than doing my head in. My children were very, very young at the time and without them knowing it, they were my saviours, in stopping me in my tracks, every time. I couldn't do that to them. I am so pleased beyond words infinite, to the moon and back that I didn't do that to them.

I have mentioned the above, to let the reader know, just how intense, penetrating and mind-blowing, the extremities of abuse and grievance like this can be and I am pleased to say since then, I have been through many healing processes and I am a lot stronger and beyond the risky, extremities I went through during that stage of my life. The many healing processes I have had in the past (and even in the now), is a letting go. I have since gained that knowledge that, deep inside of me was an abused, hurt and frightened child that needed to be recognized and she needed to be heard. Now I am acknowledging my abused, scared and frightened child and consequently, not only the journey of my many healing processes but the journey alone of writing this book has allowed me to let go off so much. I have become a much stronger, calmer and more independent woman, because of my journey. My resilience to any negative situation I have been in, has been tested to the max, even up to very recently and I have bounced back, to be able to continue with my journey, with more ease than ever before.

Start of Counselling Notes

I am going to start now, at the beginning of those notes, which I started at my counselling sessions and as mentioned before these notes will be in red type and I will fill in with black type, to help it be more understandable to the reader.

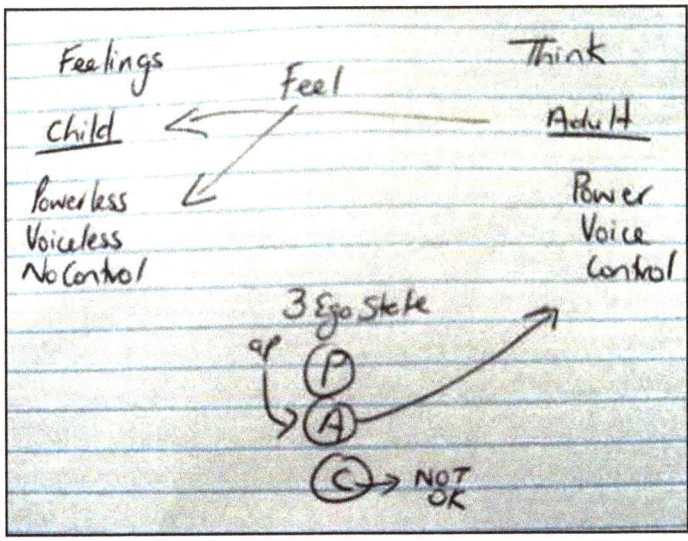

I am closing that door

25.11.10

Breaking the Silence...

I kinda of understand now... I understand now, how when I grew up, I grew up with people that let me down. People that let me down... that's what I knew... that's why I attract men in my life that let me down now. Now I am a grown woman, I attract men that let me down. Logically one might say, no way, you know different. However, psychologically I know no better. This is what I knew and this is what I know. You end up doing things that you know.

My ex-husband let me down, and was hardly there.

My present partner lets me down and is always there. When, he wasn't working and generally, there in person only.

I also kinda understand now why S.B (Initials changed). My big relative 2, grew up being told what to do, and how now as a grown man attracts people telling him what to do. He knows no better. You can see that in his religion. That religion *tells him what to do. I can see that in his wife. I'm sure she tells him what to do.*

I am now remembering his supposed friend he was telling you what to do. When he had me pinned to the ground, pinned to the ground and rubbing himself against me… he was telling you what to do… but you accepted that I suppose, because you knew no different. Because, you grew up with B.U. telling you, how to, how to what?...I'm finding this extremely hard to write, not only telling you but showing you, talking you through it… while doing it.

FUCK… HOW I HATED YOU IN THAT MOMENT

The above comment in capitals, those words were not in my notes. That is what I was feeling in the moment, as I typed those notes. I must have typed those words without realising, in the moment. It was days later, when I re-opened the file, I saw the words and thought, 'I don't remember typing that'. But then thought, oh well, it may as well stay there, as that was what I must have been feeling in the moment when I was typing those words from my notebook.

Some people out there might question here… "For God

sake, why didn't you tell someone?"

My response to that would be. When you are threatened, especially at such a young age, threatened continuously, over and over and over again, with threats like… "He will pay for it…" He is, my younger brother. "They won't believe you…" "You are not good enough…" and so on. These sayings begin to have a hold on you and the more you hear them, the more you start to believe them, especially if they are drummed in continuously. At such a young age, you learn to be silent, as you don't want this happen to you, let alone someone else, more so someone so dear to you.

I stayed silent to save my little brother; I didn't want him to suffer like I/we were. It gets to the stage that you have been silent for so long, that you learn to bury the memories. So you don't have to think about them, so you don't have to deal with them. I buried what happened to me so well; it was like it didn't happen for a long period of my life. Over the course of that period when I buried what happened to me, if a memory did surface, I would immediately stomp on it even harder, to bury it even deeper. I buried it into the depth of my Soul, deep into the abyss of my memory. At the time, not dealing with what happened to me was way easier, than dealing with something that was extremely traumatic and horrific as a child. As I said previously this intense, mind-blowing trauma from my childhood, was buried that deep, it was like it didn't happen for many years of my life.

Eventually things that you don't deal with in life, eventually rear their ugly head, so to speak, so you do have to deal with it. Memories and situations presented themselves to me in life, where I had to deal with it. I had finally come to the point, of *having* to deal with this horrific past. It got to the point that I needed to deal with, what happened to me. 'You either deal with it or you don't.' I was no exception to the rule. It was now time to deal with it, for me. That is one of the many reasons, why I am going ahead and writing this book, I want to deal with this, the best way I know how. For me, this is what I have to do.

I am going to give my Inner Child, the voice she needs, so she can come to terms with what happened to her. She needs to deal with a past that was traumatic and horrific. We both need to heal.

26.11.10

"Who would have guessed, a conversation about sport, sports of all things (I'm not really a sporty person) but a sport conversation triggered a memory. A memory, a memory of being told "you're only good for this…" Is that what I am hearing, "you're only good for this". I do try to bury that

I am closing that door

memory, but it pops up again. "You're only good for this..." I'm not sure anymore, I've buried it too quickly. But that does explain something for me, sports I have never really liked it. Always was pleased to be on the sideline, always was pleased when my hay fever played havoc. Was that because I really wasn't a sporting person, or was that because, I really did believe what my memory is (was) trying to tell me!!

This is just telling me more and more, B.U. you stole sooooo much from me. I can't say sport at the moment, as I buried that, as quickly as it came up. But I now know you stole my childhood. You stole my innocence. You stole my teenage years. You even stole my memories of my children's childhood and more, much more.

How can that be, you say, when you didn't even know me as a teenager. How can that be, when you didn't know me as an adult, especially with children. How can that be!!

I can say that about him. That he stole sooooo much from me. I still do say that. I learnt to bury the abuse, I suffered. I learnt to pretend that it didn't happen. I buried it so deeply; it was like it didn't happen. Burying what happened became a survival instinct. Blocking it out, so I didn't have to deal with it. Consequently, by doing that, burying memories that were so horrific, I ended up burying and blocking more memories, which I didn't need to.

Burying memories of something so shocking and horrific, taught me without realising, how to bury memories that were joyous and happy memories. Memories for instance, that every Mother would love to cherish while watching her children grow up. The memories a Mother loves to keep and relish and delight over, were taken from me. They were being buried, in amongst all those memories that I learnt to bury. The memories of something so shocking and horrific. It was my survival instinct.

While attending Counselling sessions, my Counsellor did warn me, that as I go through this process of being counselled about my childhood, that more and more memories from my Childhood might just surface and generally unexpectedly. When you least expect them to. I am now beginning to realise that the same is happening while writing this book, memories are resurfacing more.

That certainly did happen with me, as in the above notes from 26/11/10. I have had more like them but as I have mentioned before, out of habit, I still do end up burying

I am closing that door

them, again and again. I end up doing so, as it *is* my survival mechanism.

It was a worthy suggestion to write down what surfaced, as those memories came. It became a way to keep a trajectory, so to speak, of what was buried. As it was a way, of getting it out of my system, out of the organisms of my body. I no longer have to stomp and trudge those memories, which are written down, into the back of my memory. No longer do I have to stomp and trudge them, into the abyss of my memory. As I am typing this, there is another memory that is breaking the surface, again.

I am going to write this memory now, so I can get it out of my system. This is a memory of me as a very young girl, watching something between my legs, getting closer to where it shouldn't be. I remember the sight of this was *freaking* me out. I was gobsmacked. Even at such a young age, I knew it shouldn't be between my legs. I knew that this shouldn't be happening, that I shouldn't be witnessing what I was witnessing. But I was frozen with fear and couldn't say anything. I didn't like what I was seeing as a young child and as an adult the memory is disturbing and distressing.

Writing about those memories is allowing you, to get it out of your system and also a letting go. Now I am putting it out there what happened, once I put out there what I write, I will no longer have to bury those memories, within the abyss of my memory and Soul.

I am not saying the memories, of such an ordeal will disappear – Not at all. As in my experience, the inscription or imprint will still be there. Not stomping on those memories into the depths of my soul is a new experience. A new experience, which I'm not sure I will get used to, at this stage. I think I will get used to it.

I inevitably stomp on memories that come up, when I am not able to write them down, for whatever reason. Some memories, especially if they have resurfaced for the first time or memories that haven't re-emerged for a long time, can still do your head in. Once again, time will help, especially if you do your best to let go, either by writing them down or talk to someone about your memory or memories. If I am able to write my memories down, then at least I am able get them out there and let them go. It might not necessarily happen instantaneously either, but sooner or later, you can let go. It is definitely an idea here, to get that support from someone if possible, so you can let go in an easier manner. A problem shared is a problem halved, so they say.

Here is one of the memories, which I was never able to write down in the moment, so therefore kept forgetting. I am going to write this one, as it has just resurfaced again.

I am closing that door

Even though, this has nothing to do with any of the 3 violators, which I have written letters to in this book. I am going to mention this, to remind me, that my sister and I were also victims, of what seemed to be a complete stranger in the moment. He traumatised us with his sick behaviour as well. I am not just reminding me. But I also need to remind the reader. What might seem such a small incident and insignificant, to some people, to any other major abuse that might be happening in someone's life; it is just as traumatising and emotionally destroying as any other incident of abuse.

That night in England our parents left us children, at home alone. My sister and I were not sleepy and while in bed, we discussed and decided to create some of our own fun, in our extremely stressful childhood. We decided to hang our heads, out of our bedroom window and say hello, to anyone and everyone that walked passed. Just for the fun of it.

It was working really well; we were enjoying the freedom of just being us. It was liberating for us to be able to say hello to people passing by. We giggled and smiled at each other as each person walked by. Until, what must have been a few hours later. When this older bloke walked past and initially, he was ignoring us (now as an adult, I now realise he was actually, in an angry and irritated mood and we should have just let him walk on by, without saying anything), so we said, hello even louder and again even louder.

When we finally got his attention and he realised where the hellos were coming from, we were hoping that he would, just say hello and keep on walking – Just like everyone else, that had walked passed before him. But then, he looked behind him, from where he just came from and then looked up the street, on our side (our house was on the corner) and peered ahead of himself, where he was heading. I now realise, he was making sure there was no one else coming. He was making sure that we 2 little girls were his only audience. But we didn't realise that, at such a young age. Then he smiled, raised his eyebrows several times and proceeded to undo his belt and unzip his trousers and then started to have himself off, in front of us.

I remember the fence was partly obscuring, what he was doing. But when we, finally realised what he was, really doing. We immediately shut the windows and curtains and slung back into bed. Desperately trying to erase the disturbing and disgusting memory; amongst all the other horrific memories, that had accumulated through our childhood so far. What started as fun and liberating, ended in disgust and shame and so many other mixed emotions.

I said above, what 'seemed to be a complete stranger'. I do

I am closing that door

have that memory, in that moment... I remember thinking... I thought, that maybe I knew him, but wasn't too sure, as it was dark, but with the aid of street lights, it was possible. He could have been, one of our parents' friends' husband/partner. The name Gordon (name changed) comes to mind, but I am really not sure. If it was that Gordon, it now comes back to my memory, that he was killed falling down some stairs. I also remember, the suspicion going around at the time that the guy could have thrown himself down those stairs. As I say, that was suspicion.

My sister gave me permission to share some of her memories, to do with our childhood. I am so grateful to have her permission. This memory of hers, is to do with both of us and the more I am thinking about it, the memory is becoming a bit stronger for me (to be honest, the only one of her memories, that she told me about that I can remember, right now in this moment). I am going to write about it now and get it out there, out of my system, if I can. Then hopefully, I won't have to stomp it, back into the abyss of my memory.

My sisters' memory is, being forcibly dragged into the boys' bedroom and she is hanging onto the end of the bunk beds, in the hope that it will stop him dragging her in further into the room and trying, urgently and desperately to get herself away. She remembers our big relative 2 on top of her and my Relative 1 on top of me. The Relative 1 is describing to our big relative 2, what to do to my sister, while the Relative 1 is doing the same to me. It is only just recently, in the last few years, that I have had that memory resurface of actually being dragged forcibly into the boys' room and I was definitely fighting it. But being as young as we were, with a fully grown man (relative 1) and a big relative 2 trying to drag us into that room, we had no chance.

29.11.10

Struggling with what! I still have a 5 year old in me, trying to come to terms with what happened to her...

Not only was this young 5 year old girl violated, she was violated through-out her childhood and experienced all sorts of mixed emotions that such a young person, has no idea how to handle, her life was in extreme, turbulent turmoil.

I remember, at times that she and her siblings tried to escape their everyday life, by escaping into the Custer's Last Stand Picture on the landing. We would sit on top of the stairs and look at this picture that was hung up, to view as you come down the stairs. We would pretend that we were either at the movies, or pretend we were in that picture fighting within the scene of the Custer's Last Stand.

I am closing that door

Pretending so we could escape this continual violation, destruction and damage that we experienced. I remember thinking at times, I would be one of the Native American Indians in the picture. In my mind I would act out the dying scene of the Native American that was dying in the picture. I remember one day thinking, if I was dead like the Native American in my mind, that would be better than the life I was living now... This could put an end to my misery and despair I was in. Fantasising about being dead, numbed that extreme misery and loneliness. Thankfully that is as far, as I took those thoughts as a child. No child, especially at such a young age should be thinking of death in that way. I remember my sister and myself, more than my brother/relative 2 being on the landing looking at this picture, but the boys were there as well at times, in my memory. If they had similar thoughts, I do not know.

I remember when I was about roughly 8 maybe 9, going into my mum n dads' bedroom in England and seeing this book on the bedside cabinet and seeing the picture of a man on the front cover. I couldn't take my eyes of this young man in this picture. I just had to know who this man was, as I was enchanted in how handsome this young man looked, even at such a young age. I ended up asking her, who this man was and she told me his name and that I could have a look at this book if I wanted. I did just that and this handsome young man, who is an extremely well known entertainer, some people call him the King of Rock and Roll, became another preoccupation, another escapism or avoidance, if you like, of what I was going through as a child. I see as an adult that escaping into the handsomeness of this man was better than thinking about death. Maybe as a child I knew that too, as the times of sitting in front of the Custer picture, became fewer and fewer for me.

Over the course of time my preoccupation with this man became less and less significant. The many healing journeys that I have been on have allowed me to let go off so much. Letting go off this preoccupation of this handsome man was another letting go, many years ago now. I eventually recognized that this preoccupation was my desperate need for love and approval and at the time I had no idea of that. Any memorabilia of this man that I did have was, in the end, delivered to a true fan of this entertainer.

My escapism for the famous Movie Stars that were in the books, on the shelf in the lounge of the same house, was not as long lived as the escapism for the extremely well-known entertainer.

It is interesting to note here though, the Movie Stars within the same books of that era, was escapism for me (reverting to my childhood escapisms), when I was trying to escape the fears that I experienced, while putting of having this book published. Now though it is the Wikipedia version, which goes into way more detail about these stars, than those books ever did. Just don't get all the glamourized pictures like those books though.

2/12/10

Belief System

I'm Only Good for This

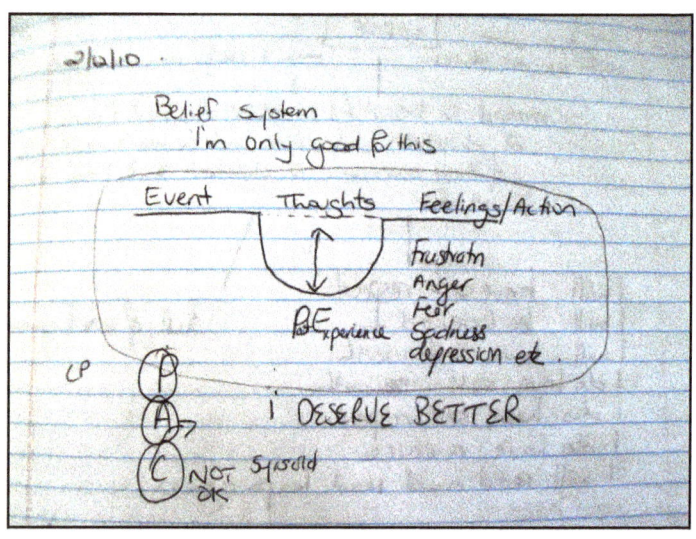

Knowledge is power

I survived. There have been many, many battles in my life and I have survived everyone, so far. I say so far, as my life isn't over yet and I know there will be more battles that I will endure. But those battles will be easier to fight than they have been in the past. I know that because I have been through many healing processes that have given me the strength to perceive and react to life differently. Not only that, I am who I am because of what I went through and have been through. I am a stronger person, because of what I went through and I have since let go off so much. I see the endeavours that I will go through in life, will be dealt with, in a way, that is a better way, then ever before. I see that more so now, since I have been made redundant from my last job.

What I achieved in spite of. There are many things I have achieved in life, in spite of what I have been through. It is worthy to think about those achievements.

I deserve self-respect. Everyone deserves self-respect.

I deserve self-worth. Everyone deserves self-worth.

I deserve to be listened to. Everyone deserves to be listened to.

I deserve to have a voice. More to the point, my Inner Child deserves to have a voice and deserves to be heard, I am giving her that voice.

I am going to have better. I know that I will have better,

I am closing that door

this is what happens when you let go off so much. I have already had better in a financial aspect, since writing this note, at least now I am not living week to week, like I used to. I can honestly say that I am now wealthy compared to my standards, in that respect. I am wealthier emotionally and spiritually. Now time will tell, with the relationship that I hope to have in the future.

I really am a good person. I consider myself a good person and some people might not see that in me. I know that might sound egotistical to some, but that is certainly not how it is meant to sound. I know I am a good person, how people perceive me though, is their choice. This is how life is and that is OK.

I'm going to take it/me back — it belongs to me. I, belong to me and no-one else.

What I Am

My Counsellor suggested making a Brainstorm of What I am or the Will Be. As per previous Brainstorm, the photo is not that clear, so I will list the centre block as the heading and list the rest underneath the heading.

Brainstorm. What I am/or the Will be

LORNE

Good mum

Handmade cushion (hand sewn)

I am lovable/loving/loved

I really am a good person

Tutor, with many success stories

Raised 2 beautiful children the best I can

2 Children who are independent, with lives of

I am closing that door

their own. 2 children that I am extremely proud of

Full of intelligence

I will have self-respect

I will be listened to

I will have self-worth

I do have self-worth

I do have self-respect

I do have a voice

I will read and read heaps again

I did leave a spare page at this stage of the exercise book, where I was taking these notes, for the inevitability of adding to this Brainstorm/Mind Map, with everything else that was going on at the time, I never went back there. If I end up adding any more to this mind map, before I finish this book, I will include it, as it is never too late. If I don't add it to this book, it will mean that this book has already been published. I will create another personal notebook and start all over again with a Mind Map, if I have to.

Telling My Children

6.12.10

I will tell my children what happened to me, but I am worried whether I should give them names or not! Even at this stage of my note taking, I still felt the need to protect the ones that hurt me. It was what I knew. I feared doing any different at this stage. I was still discovering that Lorne needs to protect Lorne, not the ones that hurt her.

I am more aware now, more things that trigger any emotion in me, it can be any innocent thing that somebody might say but I am having several emotional states during the day. Anything like sadness, anger, being unsure, feeling vulnerable, but it is just that, a trigger. I am going to get over having those triggers affect me, the best I can anyway, because I am aware that they are triggers. I didn't realise, just how long it would be, that these triggers would still distress me. Sometimes, you get so busy in life, that recognising that they are actually triggers, is easier said than done at times. This is still a work in progress, but it is getting easier and easier.

I am an intelligent woman, fully aware that these triggers can happen, but as intelligent as I am — I had no idea that they were happening to me, before my sessions! I suppose because, I buried what happened to me. I buried it sooooo deeply for along long time. In doing so, there are heaps and heaps of things that I've buried, not just bad things that have happened to me but good things, happy things. How can you B.U., how can you put me through such a horrific childhood and not only take my innocence, but you also happened to take from me much, much more, way into my adulthood. As an adult, at the stage when I was married, on an unconscious level, I even started to hide, who I was. I started to hide my first name and if anyone asked me, what is your name? I would generally say Mrs (I am now Ms) before my last name and try not to say my first name, if I didn't have to. The less I thought about my first name, I believe that on an unconscious level, that was giving me the chance to, not think about what happened to Lorne. There was a time there where I hated my first name and deep down, I think that was more to do with, that I hated what happened to Lorne, in her Childhood. Not thinking about who I was, gave me that opportunity to bury even deeper what happened to me. Now, over the course of time, I have learnt to love my first name. As unique as my name is, it is also part of the uniqueness of who I am. It is the uniqueness of me. Now I am always happy to say, Lorne, if anyone asks my name.

Well now I am going to do my best to take me back… you can't have me anymore… Another part of taking me back will be, when I get this book published (this is something that I need to do for myself – *needing* to publish a book, might not be the case for another person).

All the triggers, all the emotions, all the tears, will be worth it in the end, because I am going to have me back.

I'm actually beginning to understand now, why I'm dealing with this at this stage of my life, with all the healings I have had in the past. I actually thought I had dealt with it. Even when I saw B.U. in England, seeing him with all his ailments, knowing karma had caught up with him. I thought that visual sight was enough, but no obviously not, as it is coming out now. If I

I am closing that door

had, have dealt with it sooner, I'm sure I would have tipped over the edge. Even if I wasn't suffocated into silence and was able to let the 'Cat out the Bag' back then, when I had my melt-down, re boat trip (mentioned further along in this book) my parents' would not have had the tools to deal with this back then. The fact that they didn't have the tools to deal with this is OK with me now. *Now is the right time — now is the right time to take me back.* Now is definitely the right time to be dealing with this and take me back. Now *I am* gaining the tools to deal with this myself. *They say that healing or the healing process is like taking the layers of an onion, slowly but surely until you get to the core. I'm sure the core is where I am, if it's not, then its close. Surely.* As it turns out, there are more layers to peel before I get to the core. The core is further away than I thought, when I wrote this entry in my Counselling notes, but I am working on those layers. I am going through Self Improvement and giving myself a lot of well-deserved TLC while I can, to help me through this process.

Perhaps the other thing that I should have guessed re, *I actually thought I had dealt with it...* The other thing that should have indicated to me, that I really hadn't dealt with it, was when I visited the house, where I grew up in England. This is the same house where I spent the bulk of my life in England, the same house where my relative 1 used to babysit us in, on a regular basis.

At the new occupants' agreement, I went through the garden at Newton Rd. I saw inside the house, downstairs. Even though the new occupants didn't offer to show me upstairs, the thought of going upstairs actually made my stomach turn and feel dizzy. I didn't like the thought of going up there, I was kind of glad they didn't ask to show me upstairs. Even though another part of wanted to go up there.

If I was ever to go back to England, I hope the new occupants are gracious enough, to allow me to come back and visit that house again and that they allow me to go upstairs. If I was to go upstairs in that house and not feel sick about it. That for me would be an indication that I have gotten it, out of my system, or dealt with the horrific abuse that happened to me in that house. It would also be another healing process. Another letting go.

I did end up telling my son, what happened to me as a child. I told my son, Xmas 2010 and I told my daughter, January 2011.

I told my son *and* his partner, approx. Oct/Nov 2011 and my daughter *and* her partner, approx. Feb/Mar 2012. Knowing it was better for my children, to be able to talk to their

I am closing that door

partners, if needed. My children need no longer, keep it silent. No longer did they have to keep it to themselves. At least they had each other and their partners to talk to, if they wanted to.

It was the best thing, I could have done for myself (I thought at the time, why hadn't I done this sooner, but I also realise in that same moment, there is a right time for everything in life). I think my children held more respect for me and they realised more about their mum, then they had ever known before. I am sure it helped to explain some of their questions for them. I felt I had lifted a big liability and burden of my shoulders by telling them. I have no regrets that I told my children or their partners, as this was part of my healing process. As my children's mother, helping me in this respect was actually in turn, helping them.

Be patient with myself, be kind to myself. In the past, I certainly had been very critical of myself and had been way to busy, pleasing everyone else but myself, and this is a lesson that I needed to learn for me, that is to be kind to myself. Now is the time to focus on me and be kind to me.

This is my life — live life for me. Up till then, I had been living for everyone else in my life, forgetting that Lorne deserved to live as well. I did change that, I moved away from a relationship that was no good for me. I followed my heart and moved countries to change that. Now one of my next steps for me will be, to let go off this book.

Be proud. — Achievements in spite of. My biggest and most proud achievements are my two children that have grown into beautiful and independent adults that now have families of their own. Another achievement is the work I did as an Adult Literacy Tutor; I have many success stories in that area of my life. I am proud of those success stories. My Tutoring is a natural ability in me and my success with this has gone beyond my time as an employed Literacy Tutor. I am also proud of myself for taking on this journey of writing this book.

Positive thoughts about me

Worthy of respect — worthy of consideration

(I'm not going to be spoken to, like that)

That really hurt me. This is what I took from it and did I hear right, is that what you meant.

There have been things I wished I hadn't done, but I'm sorry.

I'M A SURVIVOR

I am closing that door

Positive sayings →

Positive actions

I have always been, as far back as I can remember, a believer in positive sayings, knowing what you put out there, and comes back to you, tenfold. I am sure these believe has helped me immensely with not only the many healing processes I have had in the past and the healing process of writing this book. It has also helped with the many other things that I have dealt with in life and is helping with just everyday life.

20/12/10

Now I'm also beginning to understand. Why! Why! B.U. I disconnected myself from my family in the U.K! I used to think it was because I was sooo young, way too young to need to have anything to do with my extended family (i.e. that was the excuse I was telling myself, at the time). *But really what was I was doing was disconnecting myself from you. From You. WHY B.U. did I have to disconnect myself from sooooo many people that I loved, that I didn't want to be disconnected from in the first place, when I left the U.K. But NZ gave the opportunity to disconnect myself from*

YOU. I did disconnect myself. It may have been a slow process, but in the end I did disconnect myself from YOU! I buried it so well; it was like it didn't happen for a long period of my life. *Unfortunately, in the end, I disconnected myself from those people in my life, that I did want something to do with. I sacrificed my extended family, just so I didn't think about YOU.*

B.U. that is another of the many, many, many things you stole from me. You stole from me my relationship with *my extended family.*

I am slowly, re-establishing a connection with some of that extended family, but it is hard with so many years gone-by, with lack of staying in touch in the first place and such a huge geographical distance and over the course of time, some of the extended family, have passed over. Even with today's technology it is easier said than done, but I will do the best I can.

23/12/10

Interestingly, I told my son this morning, interestingly because, I didn't ball into tears, telling him, as I thought I would. However I did feel the emotions well up and didn't cry till he

I am closing that door

gave me a hug.

I was able to tell him that it was a relative 1 but still couldn't say his name again; I couldn't say the relative 1 is the B.U. in this (note) book.

Relative 1 B_____, right now I, can't say or write your name at the moment. During this time, trying to say or write his name took me too close to the terrors that he put me through.

I was able to tell my son that my relative 2 sexually taunted me, and that his friend violated me — and that my relative 2 didn't know how to save me, as he didn't know how to. What I didn't tell my son is that my relative 2 had that big grin on his face... maybe I will one day.

My son promised he would let me deal with this — MY WAY.

As it turns out, I did tell my son and daughter about the big relative 2 grin, as I read them the letter, which I wrote my big relative 2. For my own healing process, I read the Big Relative 2 letter, to my children and their partners. I also read it to my sister and younger brother, as I felt in the moment; they needed their own healing process as well.

That letter, I read to them, is coming up later in this book.

6/1/11

My girlfriend texted me the other day and asked me what I got from the name she gave me. The name was _ _ _ _ _ _ / _ _ _ _ _ _ _ _ _ _ _ _ _ _ _ _, (she sometimes does this with new men in her life). I suppose because my ex-husband is known as _ _ _ _ and I used to call him _ _ _ _ _ _, when I was pissed off with him. I was utterly surprised at all the different emotions this particular text evoked in me.

I actually texted back→ _ _ _ _ u 4get I was married 2 a friggin _ _ _ _ _ _, so I get nothing at the mo, will let u know if I do!

I think she could sense the anger, stroppiness of the answer, so all she came back with was 'k'. Then I started to feel guilty at my response.

I texted her back with→ Well if that is the response I ave, just because his 1st name is _ _ _ _ _ _ that doesn't sound good! I used 2 call him _ _ _ _ _ _ if I was pissd of with him. I am actually

I am closing that door

a little surprised at my response on that 1! But maybe that is to do with what I'm going thru at the mo, re my childhood! I'm not sure, anymore? Explain next time I c u!

There were all sorts of emotions that came out that night. ____ came back with Oky dokey.

Names in above text are not typed in, out of respect for the couple concerned. I mentioned the above text in my notes, as to me it was describing how I was feeling in the moment. This needed to be added to my notes, to recollect the extreme intensity of this particular night. It didn't help that particular night, my partner at the time, was very argumentative and maybe I was taking it out on my friend, rather than the person I should have been aiming my feelings at. Once again, my partner was tapping into the psychological trauma of the unrecognized abused, wounded and terrified child within me. Getting the argumentative partner in one ear and the name of my ex-husband on the other hand, had doubled the intensity of these mixed and turbulent emotions that I was feeling this night.

The unsettling emotions brought out in me that night, were a reflection of the many, many emotions, some of those emotions, I couldn't even begin to explain and are indescribable, that I went through as an abused, distressed and frightened child.

Yesterday my friend was concerned→ she texted →u ok matey→ that also brought up emotions in me. I cried, she cared. Not many people ask me that question.

Or, so it seemed that not many people asked me that question, in that moment. Perhaps I really needed to know that message, in that moment. Thank you for sending that message to me in that moment.

26/1/11

Yesterday, I told my daughter, re my childhood, she seemed to take it well. She said "Oh my God, I never thought I would be told that today…" She gave me huge, huge hug afterwards. What did surprise me is that I didn't seem to cry as much, as when I did, when I told my son. I thought I would cry more, when I told her. Maybe that was because I already had that stepping stone with my son. Maybe that crying is yet to come.

Like my son, she did ask me what is his name, I said, "Even though I used to say his name — at the moment, I can't with what I am going through

I am closing that door

and I can't even write his name" — maybe that is yet to come as well.

30/1/11

This Australia visit has been a healing journey last night, (my daughter and her partner have done sooooo much for me), last night at Margaret River (Riverview Camp Grounds) I cried and I cried. Although I didn't want to do that here, I think that my daughter has a better idea that I have created a believe system within me, especially 'I am only good for this'. Now I am trying to get used to people giving to me, but finding it really hard and I believe it will get easier.

That night I literally cried and cried, it seemed that I couldn't stop crying, I know it was a letting go thing. It was a healing process. I had finally told both my children, they both now knew. My heart felt a lot lighter. I remember that, on that night, my heart felt a *lot* lighter.

Feeling the Fear

23/3/11 — H....

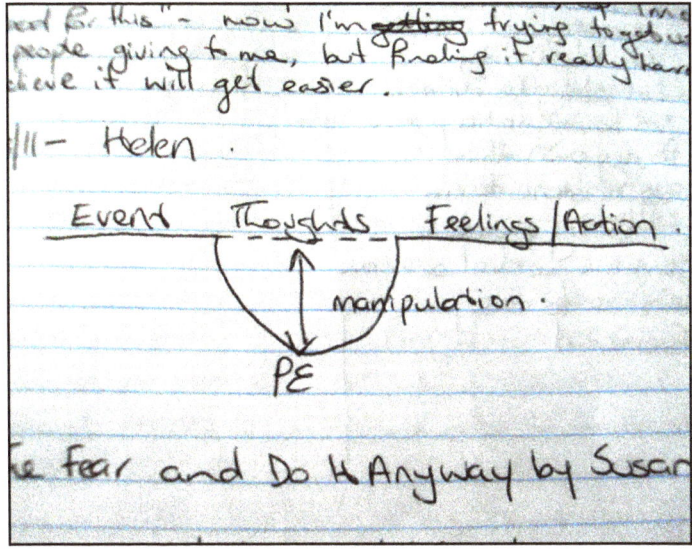

Feel the Fear and Do It Anyway by Susan Jeffers. There are other titles out there that, Susan Jeffers has written and I recommend them to anyone, who needs to 'Feel the Fear and Do It Anyway'. When it comes to '... Do It Anyway'. There have been many things I have added to that list since. There are many other self-help books out there, especially with Internet that would be available internationally.

What I will tolerate. Think about and be aware, of what I will tolerate and won't tolerate.

What I won't tolerate.

What's important for me — list it

I.e. what I need for me

Time with grandkids. My daughter was pregnant with her first, at this stage of my therapy. *Skype — internet.* I now have 3 grandbabies and one grandson is overseas with his family in NZ.

On-going education

Read more books

Walking

Teach — tech — study course. If that is what it takes!

Move house. Not only did I move house, I have since moved countries. The house I am in at present is not the last house I will be living in.

Time for myself

Time with the ones that are my nearest and dearest

To feel respected

To be loved/loving/lovable

To feel rewarded

To be able to help and be supportive to others

To be fulfilled

To have a voice

To be heard or listened to

To have self-respect

To have self-worth

To continue being the good person I am

To continue being the best mum and grandparent☺, I possibly can

To continue being supportive in helping people in their journey, with more success stories to tell

Laughter

I am closing that door

To have on-going education

To work in a friendly environment

Meet new friends

To read and read

To travel

To have an occupation that I am passionate about again

To have an occupation that will allow me to save money

To have an occupation that will fit into my lifestyle

To have an occupation where I can use my natural skills

Have an occupation that is interesting and keeps me busy enough never to get bored

The additions in black type, I have added since I took those counselling notes. I could add more to this list, but I think you get the idea now that as you progress through this healing process, it enlightens you more.

Make a Goal

Make a Goal

Pros of leaving:

Alone

Not answer to anyone

No grieve

No negativity

Not seeing his dramas

Not having to keep the peace

Do my own thing

Stepping stone to my healing process

No more control over me

I am closing that door

Be true to me

Financial

Cons of not leaving:

Be passive aggressive

Being a doormat

Ostracized

Meat in sandwich scenario

Finance!!

There is more that I could add to this list now. The Pros that I have felt since leaving are numerous beyond words. There is more that I could even add to the Cons, but once again, if I was to add more to the above, the Pros would still far outweigh the Cons. The peace of mind that I have experienced for not being in the above situation was not foreseeable back then, how immeasurable that is now. I am not going to add to the Cons list, as I am not in that situation anymore and don't need to put my thoughts back there. Here are just *some* of the Pros, which could be added to the above list:

Peace of mind

Being my own person

Travel

Freedom

Personal growth on an emotional, physical and spiritual level

Letting go off not just baggage from the above situation, but therefore being able to let go off more baggage from my past

Being able to find out who Lorne, really is – She has always been a nice person, so I have been told, but now there are traits there that maybe were there at the beginning but now more of her is being revealed, as to who she really is.

Letter to Relative 1

You will see below that, at this stage of my counselling I am able to write his name. Even though, it is a formality in addressing him. I was able to write the name of one of my violators, in my life. Being able to write his name is a big step for me, at this stage of my Counselling. Please tolerate relationship status and name change.

Could write the following in a card and send to him...

Relative 1 Bert, (that's what I used to call you).

I know what you did...

I know you violated me from 5 years of age

I know what you did...

I know you raped me from 5 years of age

I know what you did...

I know I wasn't the only one…

What I went through was horrific, horrifyingly horrific

No one person should have to go through what I went through

I'm not going to keep the peace anymore…

Raped, Raped, Raped, Raped — over and over again

Loss of innocence, loss of innocence,

Loss of memories, loss of memories and much more

Loss, loss, loss, loss and more loss

I need to deal with it…

You took sooooooo much from me…

I know I wasn't the only one…

By giving you this, I'm taking me back

I'm not keeping the peace anymore…

I need to deal with it

I am closing that door

So I'm telling you…

I know what you did…

Your Relative LORNE

Write name backwards and then tear it up. Whether it is a perpetrator or partner that is abusive.

When visiting my younger brother 10/10/11, I read him the letter that I wrote above. I told him, that I hadn't posted it to the relative 1, but intended to include it in the book, that I knew I was about to write.

It was my younger brother's suggestion, that I put the letter in a stamped envelope and address it to Relative 1 Bert, and if I didn't want to put the real address on it, to put a Mock Street name and Mock City, etc. and post it. Or put the message in a bottle to the sea. Just so I have that action of giving, but give it to 'Relative 1 Bert'. Therefore, having that action of actually giving it to him and physically, letting go off it, which in turn, will be another healing process.

I imagine when this book is published, that if the right person was to read this book. That person, once they have figured out who this Relative 1 is, would more than likely go knocking on his door. I don't have to physically give him this letter; they would be doing that on their own accord, if that was to happen.

As time has gone past, I now feel I need to do that action of giving this letter to him, so I can physically let go. Today (4/3/13) I have put this letter on paper (refill), once again as per the above letter and sealed the envelope. I even put my name at the bottom of the letter. I have decided to address the envelope, with the Mock Address. As you can imagine, I haven't put a Senders Address on it, as I don't want it returned to me. I don't want that letter back in my hands, at all.

Even though this is actually a mock address, I decided to include the mock address, here. There does seem to be clues within this address, whether intentional or not. It tells the County, I was last aware that he used to live in (maybe he still does) and it has a clue to where we lived and similar road name, as to where he used to live. I no longer have his real address, as he moved north, as far as I am aware, not long after I left the UK, when I visited.

Relative 1 Bert
49 Toddards Road
Newton-Upon-Thames
Littlies
Essex
ENGLAND, RM757549

I am closing that door

I will apologise in advance, for any inconvenience I might cause the Postal Service. But OMG… today 28/3/13, I posted the letter, with the mock address. It was two walks up to letter box, mind you. On the first walk to the letter box, I posted the first letter (which was a business letter). I walked back to where the ATM is, thinking I just need a moment before posting the Relative 1 letter and found the ATM was out of service. I went straight back to the letter box and posted the Relative 1 letter. Just like that – It was, almost like posting any other ordinary letter. The only difference was I was conscious of the fact that, once I let go of the letter, into that slot… I opened my hand, which was my right hand… really wide. The sigh of relief was massive. There is no turning back now. I did expect to be standing at that letter box for ages, before I had the courage to let go and I did wonder if I would let go! It was easier than I thought it was going to be. Once I let go, phew – such a big phew. The Postal Service now holds within the system, this letter that has a mock address on it. I can tell you that the letting go off that letter was immense though. It was a mammoth thing to do. Actually physically letting go off something, that was so brutal and horrendous in my childhood was a huge sigh of relief, it was liberating. I am still having huge sighs of liberation, as I type this entry into my book. Once again, I apologise to the Postal Service for any inconvenience.☺☺

I know at this stage, I will not be posting the letter to the real address, as I don't know the real address and I still don't think I need to. But if that changes, for instance, if I found out the real address and decided to send the letter, to the real address, I wonder if it will be that easy. I think it will be easier, in fact I think it will be liberating, now I have had that experience of putting the letter, with the mock address into the Postal system.

7/4/11

Consider

What the worse of the 2 evils

I would be free to be me

Redundancy

Possible border

Keep the peace

How about rocking the boat

Consider what the consequences are

Get past that feeling I am on a time limit. 23.6.13
– I have just realised, I still do that at work. I put myself on a time limit, even though that is partly, what my present

work has been about, time limits, but works time limits. My work situation is kind of reflective of, what I put myself through in the past. I don't need to put myself on time limits – working with works time limits, is one thing. Putting me on a time limit is another. This comment also refers to outside of work hours.

+ get past that feeling that I need to please him.
He was fortunate enough to have selected a woman that was, still in the habit of being true to her old pattern.

Perhaps I should be wholly truthful with his negativity → i.e. that I don't like his temper and his negativity

Develop balls. Unconsciously I was still at this stage of repeating an old pattern from my childhood, following that old pattern of submission and silence or *Keeping the Silence.*

I've been to a meeting → I don't want hear it → get used to it, there is more to come.

Write to Tokoroa guy (a letter)

Perhaps write down appearances (if I remember)

It has ruled my life up till now → now I'm cut-

ting this off... etc.

Write to entity

Link that breaking the link with SB and breaking the link with JP as well. (Initials changed).

I hate it, when you get negative. I don't like it→ I'm not going to put up with it → walk out if necessary, even if it's only round the block.

As it turns out, to date I haven't yet, written the letter to the Tokoroa Entity into my Counselling notes. I wrote to him on refill and because of the high, unsettled and intense emotions I was experiencing at the time, my writing was becoming very erratic. I stopped and thought I would redo that letter, at a later stage and then put it into my Counselling notes.

His facial features are hard to remember, maybe that memory of his looks, will come back when I write that letter into my Counselling notes, then again, maybe not.

I call him Tokoroa Entity, as I can't remember his actual name; I have no other name to call him but Tokoroa Entity. I feel that adding that letter to my Counselling notes, is yet to come while writing this book (which will be another healing process for me and my Inner Child – and others I am sure). It's just taking longer than I thought. But it will come later in this book (how is that for positive thinking).

20/4/11

It wasn't my fault and I don't need to feel guilty, re the abuse.

Cutting off those habitual thoughts. These are the habitual thoughts that were created, during my childhood.

I am now going to change those thoughts. I do sometimes find myself, still in those habitual thoughts, but when I realise that I am thinking them, I do my best to cut those thoughts off.

It makes me a stronger person

Start exercising being an adult and not letting those childhood thoughts come through that created the pattern for me, because of what I went through.

I'm not that person anymore. I am a stronger person since going through, not just this healing process but all the other healing processes I have gone through in the past.

I'm me. I am unique, there is only one me. That makes me very distinctive.

Celebrate me. With what I have been through, not just the battles I have fought but the achievements I have made. I have decided that is worth celebrating.

Celebrate the battles I have fought. There have been plenty of battles that I have fought. My life has been full of battles. Once you have come through any battle, it is worth celebrating. Now I have come this far and let go off so much, I believe the battles I will have to fight in my life will be fewer and fewer. That is a nice thought. The next battle is to now finish this book and let go off this. When it is out there, you will know that I have achieved this battle as well☺.

Celebrate the good changes I've made. There have been plenty of good changes that I made within my students lives as a Tutor and I loved to see the smile on their faces, when those good changes occurred☺. There also have definitely been good changes in my life. Now I live in Perth, Australia (which ended up being the perfect place to write this book). I have more interaction with 2 of my grandchildren now I am here. I also have the capability to go on the occasional holiday to see my other grandbaby in New Zealand. To me, by my standards, I am wealthier than I ever used to be. I am wealthier emotionally, physically and spiritually. I am stronger (wealthier) than I ever used to be I am sure.

I am closing that door

Keep looking at what I want to do

Setting goals for now and future

Intend to finish letter to Entity

24th – Feel the Fear

Leave my partner

My papers for work. I did succeed in passing these papers for my work at the time – another succession in my life.

Intend to talk to both brother and relative 2.

I say both, as for my little brother, I felt I needed to explain that, it wasn't his fault. I believed that my younger brother had hidden his own memories, from hearing what I/we (when I say we, I mean my sister and myself) went through.

I felt that he needed to heal his own past, as well. My younger brother was in the household, when this disturbing, horrific abuse was happening. I believe he must have heard something. Even though I/we were doing my/our best to keep silent, as I/we feared, my/our younger brother would suffer like us. No matter how silent we were trying to be, we made noise. I remember my Relative 1 putting his hand over my mouth, to muffle the noise I was making, while I was crying and sobbing for him to stop. Deploring and sobbing that he was hurting me. My younger brother must have heard something and hearing that sort of thing, would have been, very disturbing and traumatic.

As for my big relative 2, I knew I needed to confront him as well. I was prepping/psyching myself up to read him the letter, that had taken me soooo long to write.

4/5/11

Don't be in a hurry to talk to relative 2. When I am ready

Be prepared for slap down

When I feel right about it, don't push it...

Chunky crayons and piece of paper

Whatever I want to put on that paper

Doesn't have to make sense

Therapy to draw, whatever makes sense

Pastel – spray with hairspray to make it stick

Book – author Ruth ? H..... will lend me

I am closing that door

I did read that book, mentioned above and it was helpful in my journey, when I was ready to give it back to my counsellor – she actually ended up giving me that book. She had ended up with another copy for herself. That book is still in my possession. Thank you. The book is called 'Encounters with Grace' by Ruth Penny.

Pictures

I am going to put the pictures here which I drew, with colouring pencils and felts (which were the only tools, I had available in the moment), that night, re the above notes. My counsellor had suggested at one stage and maybe even that session just mentioned, that drawing is a good release of emotion and even if you can't draw, just write what comes to mind or even if it turns out to be just a doodle, it will help to express your feelings in that format.

After drawing these pictures, I immediately put them away that same night. The night I drew these pictures, the process brought up a lot of emotion and heaps of other feelings, which are generally indescribable. I cried and cried this night as well.

I didn't pull these pictures out, until I was getting them ready for this book. These pictures will be in order that I drew them. I must admit, getting them ready for this book did bring up emotion. Emotion and sensations no doubt, which still needed to be released. I am sure that there will be more emotional releases, before I have finished this book, but it will be worth it, I need to give this a voice, not just for me but also my Inner Child.

Sure enough, when and what makes you emotional or will make you cry or experience other emotions at times, when you least expect it, definitely happens. It's just like the Facebook News Flash of Madeleine McCann, which I saw on 18/1/13. Luckily, I was home alone at the time. I didn't even get to read the post. I just looked at Madeleine's face and burst into tears. News of Madeleine going missing happened, when I was travelling to England. It was all fresh news when I arrived. There goes that connection to England again for me. Seeing Madeleine's face on Facebook was an emotional release for me.

With my pictures, I want the reader to see the rawness of the moment, to let them know that showing emotion or feelings in this format is OK. You can tell by the way, my words were written, so erratically and the scribble within the pictures shows the confusion and anger I was feeling, at the time. It also shows the arguments I was having within myself, at the time.

The above picture is just scribble and that is all it is, I remember being angry, and that was the only thing I could draw in the moment. Pen/pencil and paper is definitely a good release and it doesn't have to make sense.

I am closing that door

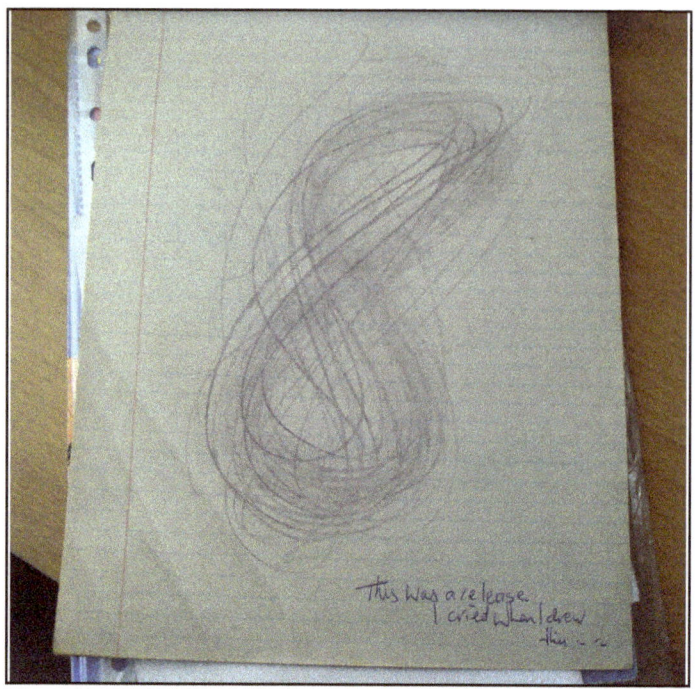

In the above pic, I was still angry, but at least the anger was more direct, it ended up being the figure 8. I wrote at the bottom, at the time. This was a release, I cried when I drew this.

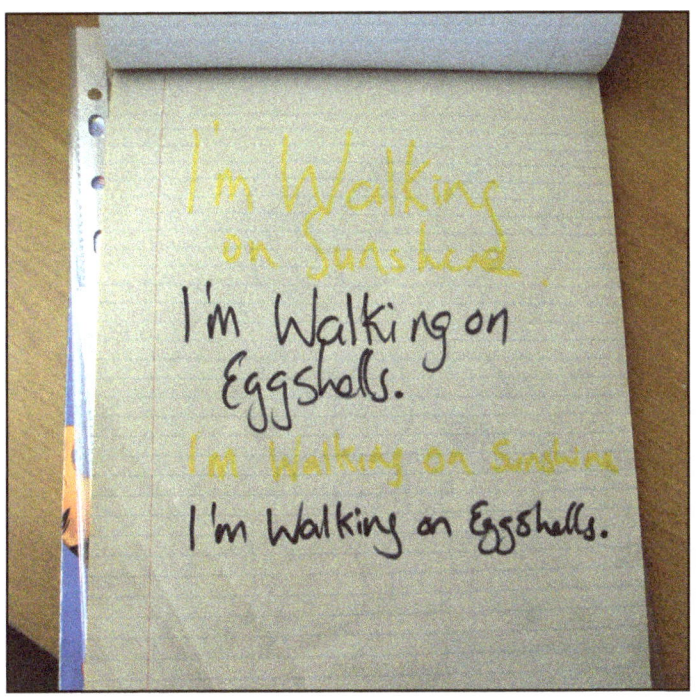

The above says it all. My writing says, there is a lot of confusion and having to be careful of what I said (re: eggshell comment). But my picture is depicting hope as well, by talking about sunshine.

I am closing that door

Confusion in amongst more confusion, question marks galore and even backward question marks in amongst all those tears and within those tears, some really heavy tears, as well. I really did need to get this out of my system.

Is life truly a beginning

Or is life truly an end, is what I wrote in amongst that spiral at the top of the picture and now that word beginning with L in the middle of the picture doesn't make any sense to me anymore and probably is just that, scribble.

I am closing that door

The faint writing at the top of the picture says – can you predict what's going to be or can you not – and just in case you can't see or understand the rest, I wrote

If life is the beginning

What is the end

Can you tell me

Or is it that the end is the beginning

who am I to say

Life is the beginning and the end.

Life is the End and the beginning→ can you tell – how are we supposed to know →

Underneath the trees I wrote – How are we supposed to know – can you tell.

The trees that I drew, are telling me, that there is growth, but also windswept thoughts.

I am closing that door

This is a merry-go-around, is what I wrote, in amongst the circular shape at the top of the picture

The number Eight is haywire

As you can tell, there is still a lot of emotion still happening within my drawings.

Why is it a merry-go-around. Then if number Eight is haywire

88888

88888888

You can't tell can you

Of course I can tell.

You can't tell can you

I am closing that door

Of course I can tell

You can't tell can you

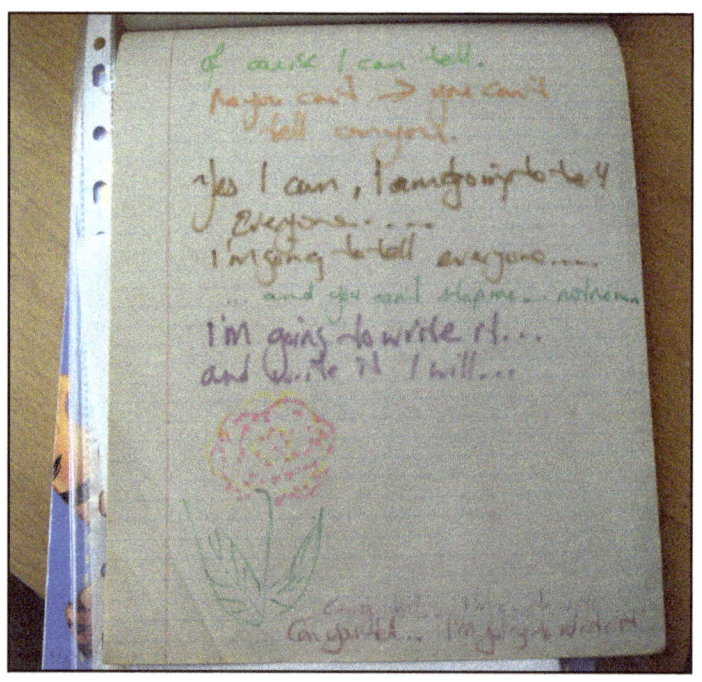

Of course I can tell

No you can't → you can't tell anyone.

Yes I can, I am going to tell everyone...

and you can't stop me... not now... I'm going to write it...
And write it I will...

And by that flower that I drew, which depicts growth to me, I wrote –

Can you tell… I'm going to write it

Can you tell… I'm going to write it.

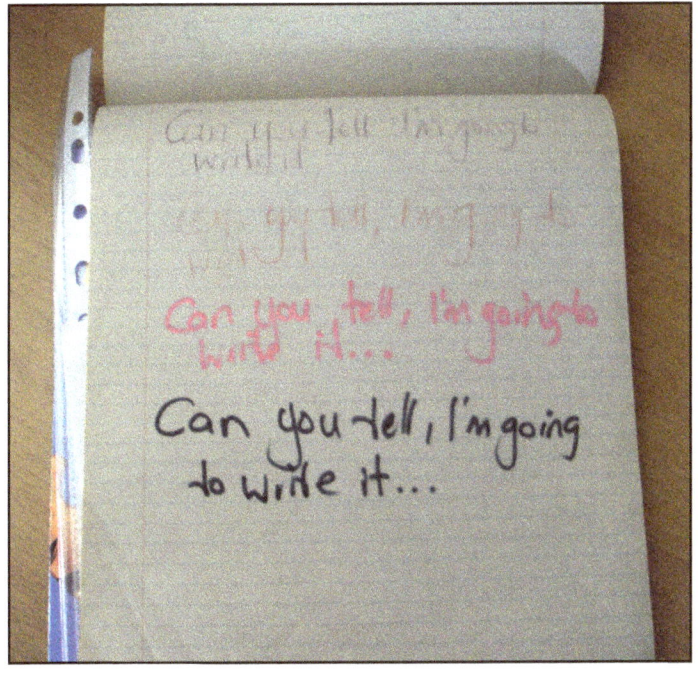

Can you tell I'm going to write it

Can you tell I'm going to write it

Can you tell I'm going to write it…

I am closing that door

Can you tell I'm going to write it...

So then I drew this red face, with lots of red hair hair -deep red hair and tore it up...

I need to let go...

I will write it to let go.

And let go I will...

And by that flower that I drew, which depicts growth to me, I wrote –

Can you tell… I'm going to write it

Can you tell… I'm going to write it.

Can you tell I'm going to write it

Can you tell I'm going to write it

Can you tell I'm going to write it…

I am closing that door

Can you tell I'm going to write it...

So then I drew this red face, with lots of red hair hair -deep red hair and tore it up...

I need to let go...

I will write it to let go.

And let go I will...

Why is it a merry-go-around. Then if number Eight is hay-wire

88888

88888888

You can't tell can you

Of course I can tell.

You can't tell can you

I am closing that door

Of course I can tell

You can't tell can you

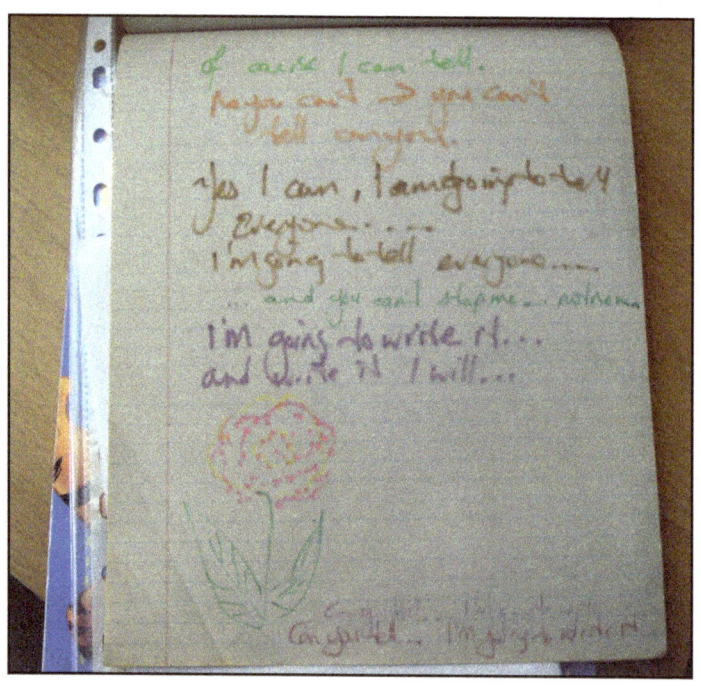

Of course I can tell

No you can't → you can't tell anyone.

Yes I can, I am going to tell everyone...

and you can't stop me... not now... I'm going to write it...
And write it I will...

Boat Trip

The brief mention of the boat trip below is an incident that happened, when we had been in New Zealand for a year, maybe less. That same Relative 1 came to visit us in NZ. When we found out this Relative 1 was coming to NZ, I do remember spinning out within myself, but also remember thinking, I can't let this show, and I can't let them know. The fear that was so ripe in England. The fear which I hadn't had time to get over came flooding back, big time. It gripped me into suffocation. Once again, feeling so alone, as I couldn't express what I wanted to say. What I needed to say stayed covered up and buried, even deeper.

During this visit, from that same Relative 1, I can't remember where we were. I think we were holidaying somewhere in the South Island. We, the kids, all of us, as an 11th hour organization, were to go on a boat trip with this Relative 1. I tried to get out of it, right at the last minute. I tried to tell my parents, more so my Mum (I remember my dad standing in the background, against an outside building – I remember my dad was hesitant in stepping forward to help his daughter who rarely threw tantrums, but I realise

I am closing that door

as an adult, he didn't want to rock the boat. He was the peacemaker in the family, this is what he knew. He didn't know how to step forward and help in these circumstances, and that is OK), why I didn't want to go on this boat trip, but all I could do front of everyone, is plead that I didn't want to go then she said, I had to go. I pleaded and begged with her not to make me go and the more I pleaded and begged, the more she said no, you have to go.

Eventually the look on her face told me that I should get on that boat or suffer the consequences. I was just about to throw a bigger tantrum and tell my mum why I didn't want to get on this boat, but before I did, I turned around and saw my sister and little brother on the boat waiting and thought about the past in England. I then thought of the possible detriment, my sister and younger brother could come to. Being shocked and terrified for them and for me, I immediately got onto the boat. I needed to be there, just in case I had to save them. Consequently, I ended up once again, burying my fear, burying all the extreme emotions that were resurfacing, once again, into the depths of my soul, into the abyss of my memory. These extreme emotions stayed buried for such a long time.

I have wondered since I have become older that maybe this Relative 1 had decided that he might come over to apologise. If that was his purpose, he never did. What I do remember though is the look on his face, once I got onto that boat; it was a look a relief. I am sure though, it was a look of more, ok I got away with that one, rather than phew she got on the boat after all.

Think about needing to be there for my sister→ re boat trip

Hurting someone else is hurting me.

I need to be. I need to be, so I don't hurt myself anymore.

That same night I wrote this

Misuse of trust

Misuse of trust

Hurt

Hurt

Devastated

Devastated

Bewildered

Bewildered

I am closing that door

Shattered

Shattered

Exposed

Exposed

Let down

Let down

Guilty

Guilty

Gobsmacked

Gobsmacked

Angry

Angry

Hate

Hate

Grief

Grief

Disappointment

Disappointment

Shame

Shame

Disgust

Disgust

How can you expect a 5 year old to deal with all those emotions?

How can you expect a 5 year old to deal with all those emotions?

Did you start on me before I was 5 — is that why I felt the need to save…

Did you start on me before I was 5 — is that why I felt the need to save…

Is that why I needed to save…

Is that why I needed to save…

I am closing that door

You put me in that position to choose!

You put me in that position to choose!

I was 5 when you put me in that position to choose

I was 5 when you put me in that position to choose

The position to choose, that he put me in when I was 5. I remember he had just dressed my sister. It must have been just after bath time. He took my sister to my parents' room and then said to me "you go on downstairs and join the boys…" and then he closed the door. Being so young at the time, I still knew this was wrong. I knew there was nothing right about the action that had just taken place. So, I insisted that I go in the room. He opened the door ajar and he still said, no. He repeated what he said above and closed the door again. I was beginning to feel more and more afraid, terrified, petrified and troubled for my sister, so I threw a tantrum and he had no choice, but to let me in my parents' room. I knew I didn't want him harming my sister. I believe he manipulated it that way, to get me into to my parents' room with so many different mixed unsettling emotions. Once I was in that room, instead of putting his attention on my sister, he turned his attention towards me. I even remember the words, "Ok, you asked for it..." and I remember him reaching between my legs towards my knickers. I have blocked the rest, maybe that memory will become clearer, maybe it won't, maybe that memory is better of buried.

Another memory I will write about here, especially as it has resurfaced, while writing about the above.

My relative 1 had both us girls on the edge of the bed and he was touching me inappropriately, in areas he shouldn't have been, once again. I remember looking to my right and realised, my older relative 2 was looking on. I even remember my initial thought, yeah, he will stop this and I even remember indicating to my relative 2 with a look, that we are not enjoying this, please help! Then my Relative 1 says, "Here you go Shaun (name change), this is how you do it..." Then I remember, my relative 2 smiling. I remember being flabbergasted and shocked and suffering all sorts of other emotional turmoil, realising my big relative 2 wasn't about to save us and our relative 1 was about to put us through more torment.

18/5/11

I have to do this for me!!

Who protects LORNE?

How can LORNE protect LORNE?

I am closing that door

I have the power

I need to protect LORNE

LORNE needs to protect LORNE

Challenge my thought patterns. I'm an adult

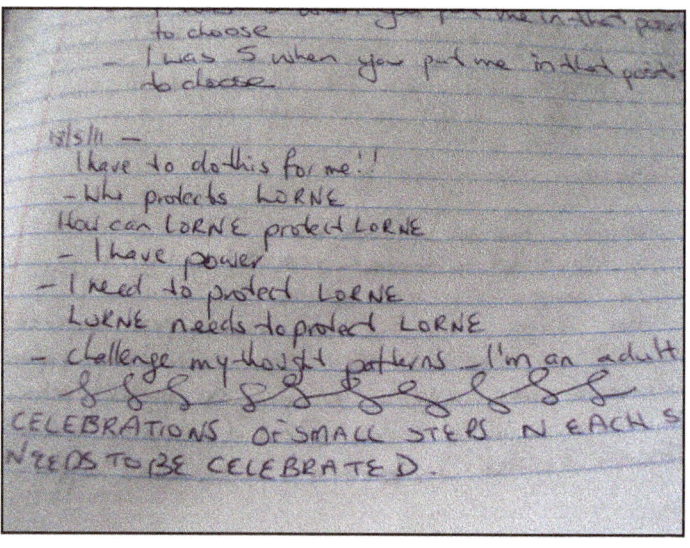

CELEBRATIONS OF SMALL STEPS AND REMEMBER EACH STEP NEEDS TO BE CELEBRATED.

I have included the above picture in this book because not only was this a doodle in the moment, within my counselling notes, but this is one of the many patterns that was taught in school when they were teaching us how to write (joined up writing). My sister made a comment, a few years ago now, that she remembers years ago that I always used to do this pattern, especially this pattern, when I could. To me this was escapism, yet again.

1/6/11

L... (Little sister), you don't need to feel guilty, because I didn't save you last time, it certainly wasn't your fault, just as it wasn't for me

(save and save)

And why I couldn't save you last time

Perhaps write it, perhaps read it, but don't necessarily read it to her.

Unknown quantity – be sure about my direction

Getting it out there, as destructive inside me. This is within the time frame that I decided to write this book. It is not until I visited my Australian Osteopath, that I learnt just how destructive this was to my body. His words were on this first visit that holding onto this book is killing you, if you do not let go off it (in my case, I had taken most of this emotion in my stomach area). I am now determined to let go off this book, so I can get it out there. His words actually scared me back into action. I am determined that this destruction is not going kill me.

The abuse was the problem. Not me.

Put it on the table and its there. It, being the abuse.

The problem isn't me, it's the abuse

My whole aim is to get well and heal and get rid of this heaviness. Keeping this abuse bottled up inside is destructive and harmful to my body, as above it is very detrimental to me, if I hang onto this book. Another way to let go off this, is to tear or burn a hardcopy of this, but in my case, I need to get this book published.

Park it on the table till one day, I will come and look for it and it won't be there!

22/6/11

Relaxation time at night time…

Don't let him make me feel guilty

In a hypa aroused state. This is referring to him and me.

He taps too much into my past experience. He taps into the physiological trauma of the abused, wounded and terrified child within me.

Through all of this I've been too busy protecting everyone else. Who is going to protect me?

I'm getting exhausted. (consider anti-depressants, takes 3 weeks to kick in). See what happens!!!

Read books, drink water, scrabble, word games, crosswords, things that I like and can manage. Play music, watch family movies, laughter is good for the soul. Do what is good for me.

Thankfully, it didn't get to the stage, of needing to take anti-depressants, mentioned above. Or was it, that I was strong enough, I realised I could go through, what I was going through, without the aid of drugs. Whichever it was, I'm so glad that I didn't take anti-depressants, as I didn't want to become dependent on drugs. I also knew that taking drugs would make my journey harder to overcome.

Silently Screaming

27/6/11

I now know what I silently screamed to myself, way back then. I have just discovered another pattern I have created in my life!!... I screamed for someone to come and save me... I screamed it to myself → now my sister is coming to my rescue.

The above, is referring to the time mentioned in my Big Relative 2 letter ... *In that moment I crawled into the deepest, darkest place I could find...* On the day that I wrote my entry on 27/6/11, I finally remembered what it was, I was screaming on that occasion. I was screaming for someone to come and save me. I remember screaming, screaming and screaming it out. But it came out silently, each time. It came out unheard, each time. It came out unheeded, each time. In that moment back then, I so desperately needed to be saved, by anyone that would come and take me away from this place at Elizabeth Dr, just anyone. I basically didn't care who it was, that might come and save me from this major torment that I was is in. When I heard my parents come home though, I immediately swallowed those screams. I swallowed them into the depth of my soul. I swallowed them deep into the abyss of my memory. I didn't want to tell them, I didn't want to tell them because of the threats and intimidations that had been drummed into us by our Relative 1. I didn't want to tell them for the *fear of the unknown*. There was copious fear in us then, we just couldn't tell.

As that memory only resurfaced on that day in 2011, it seemed ironic that at the time I was in a situation, many years later, after silently screaming what I did. I needed to be rescued from a relationship that was no good for me, a connection that was hostile for me. It was a bond that kept my Inner Child as wounded and just as terrified as she was back then. My sister rang me this night and told me, she was offered the use of a vehicle, which was perfect to shift me to another house, during this period of time. Finally, it seemed in the moment, that the Universe responded to my screaming pleas, many years later. Someone was finally coming to *my* rescue. Finally someone was coming to save me from the torment I was going through. I love my sister profoundly for that. The tears I cried that night were incalculable, another expressive release, amongst the many others.

The below letter is a letter I wrote, with his suggestion,

I am closing that door

to my partner at the time. Little did he recognize in the moment he suggested, I write this letter, he did me a massive favour. As what I wrote him, helped me realise that this had been happening all my life. This was part of me exposing parts of what I had been through in the past, as well. This was another pattern that I had been allowing, to happen to me. This letter needed to be added to my counselling notes, to remind me never, never to let that happen to me, ever again.

Why I need to leave

To deal with way back then

No more verbal attacks on

Me

My kids

My family

My friends

My work

My cat

And much more

No more continuously *listening to negatives day in and day out*

I'm tired

I need to be happy. I need to be me

No more assumptions and accusations

No more broken promises

No more threats

No more protecting those ones that hurt me, incl. way back then

There is one more thing that I will share here, re the above letter. Not that I will write out the whole letter, but I will take out extracts of this letter. This other letter helps describes, what I was feeling during that period in my life, feelings which are my feelings. Maybe a reader might recognise the same or similar within themselves. These extracts come from another letter that I wrote, around that same time factor, approx. 7/11.

Extracts of letter:

…you say you are going to change… but I can't take the chance anymore … I can't take the chance that I will be

I am closing that door

hurt again… I haven't got it in me anymore to give to that… I have given sooo much to that… I don't want to be wondering anymore, when the next incident might happen. I would always wonder…

… I have now just realized that I have been wondering *all* my life, when might the next 'incident' happen… whatever that 'incident' might be…

… I do intend to get over what happened to me way back then and I can't do that while people are still hurting me… or while I'm still wondering when the next 'incident' might happen….

6/7/11

Today is the 13th session, 3 more to go

Concentrate on what's good for me

Muscular tense and relax, when trying to sleep

Breaking the Silence → say what I want to say (Breaking the Silence was a name, I was considering for my book, at this stage).

Take courage with this book and my future endeavours.

Need to go within what I feel. I need to be me

The world is my oyster — I'm free to choose to be able to do what I want to do

24/8/11

Think about the what if's, could go into denial (re S.B. big relative 2) look at what I've got

Kinda of relationship — risk losing it altogether totally → or some sort of reconciliation

Telling him in a letter

Him recognising and admitting wrong

Him totally denying

Him seeing it from a different point of view

Put it behind me and move on. Depending on how it goes

I don't have to rescue everybody

I can now live my own life

I am now an adult

I don't have to be the captivity of my past. Writing

I am closing that door

this book and putting it out there will allow me more, to not be captive of my past.

What I do want, I want to achieve — I can achieve

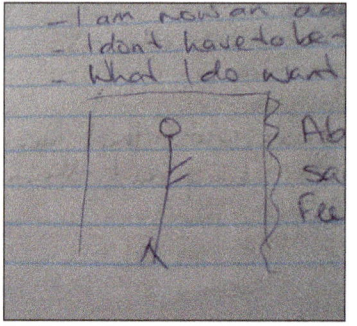

Abuse

Sacrifice

Feeling of having to rescue everyone

Keep on working to bring change and different choices

This is the 1st day of the rest of my life (remember there will be the triggers)

The thoughts can be there, but you don't have to let them linger

The Big Relative 2 Letter

The below letter took such a long time to write (penned). I wrote and redrafted and rewrote this letter, many times. I tore up the old versions of the letter, each time I redrafted it, which was very therapeutic, as I was tearing up the past, as many times as I revised the letter.

I wanted to make sure I put on paper as much as I could, to the best of my ability. Wanting him to know to the best of my ability, just how deeply my childhood and what my relative 2 did, affected me.

I needed it written down, as I finally came to the realisation, I wouldn't be able to tell him everything in the moment that I needed to tell him everything. I am so glad I did it in letter form, as I was able to tell him everything I wrote in the letter. As this was part of my counselling/healing process, I also decided that this letter needed to be in my counselling notes and rewriting it out once again, was still yet, another letting go off the past process.

You will see, when reading the letter I wrote my relative 2, that I am finally able to write the Relative 1's name within the letter, not just as a formality, addressing him at the beginning of the letter, that I wrote to the Relative 1. To me, this is showing that there is progress with the healing of my past.

I eventually got to see my relative 2, to read him this letter, on the eve of my 50th birthday. I sat and read the letter, which was on refill out loud to him, which was not in front of his wife. After reading him the letter, I gave him the opportunity to keep the letter or I would take it home. Initially he wanted me to take the letter, but he ended up snatching it out of my hand and keeping it, saying he wanted to read it for himself. I hope he did take the time to read it for himself. I hope that he read it and took it from my point of view, as I saw it.

Reading this letter to him on the eve of my 50th birthday (I turned 50 in Sept. 2011), goes to show, how long it took for me to come to terms with, what my Relative 1 and he put me through, growing up as a child. I am yet to fully come to terms with what his supposed friend put me through. To date (3/2/13), I still haven't been able to add that letter into my Counselling notes.

Maybe I am yet, to come to the realisation, as I have overcome so much since then, that might be all it takes, to come to terms with what the Tokoroa Entity did and that

I am closing that door

is, to do just that, just add it to my counselling notes.

What happened to me as a child, I needed to deal with it, so I could get on with life, as well as heal my Inner Child. I also felt I needed to read it to him before I turned 50. I wanted to go, into the next half a century of my life feeling freer and unhampered, which would enable me to move forward with my life. Just got in by the skin of my teeth, but I did it, before I turned 50.

To My Big Relative 2…

There was a time, when you doted on me…

There was a time, when I looked up to you…

There was a time, when I screamed and screamed my lungs out, so hopefully someone would come and save you and me…

That was the time when you were beaten up for a weeks' worth of lunch money in the park, on the way to school…

I was roughly 5 when that happened… I felt helpless… but no one came to your rescue→ no one came to my rescue, at the park.

That time, when I looked up to you, was a very short-lived part of my life…

How could I look up to someone who was there, but couldn't save me➔ who didn't try to save me or my little sister➔ didn't save us➔ no longer did I look up to you…

I was the one that was put in the position, of having to save my little sister… I was there to save my little sister…

I did that by sacrificing myself➔ to save my little sister…

Sacrificing myself to the one that should have protected me, not only me, he should have protected us… as he was the supposed adult… He let me down… He let you down… He let us down…

I was put in the position of being the protector at roughly 5 years of age… I ended up protecting my little sister and my little brother many, many more times… He manipulated it so… He, being Relative 1 Bert… He abused me sooo… he raped me sooo… He also manipulated you… He

I am closing that door

manipulated you to be the abuser as well...

You became the sexual taunter... You taunted me sexually...

So I grew to hate you more and more... I hated you soooo much...

I continuously was the protector... I no longer looked up to you... looking up to you, died, when I sat there and I realised you weren't going to try and save, what was about to happen... that was one of the times when I sacrificed myself to protect my little sister...

At such a young age of being the protector, I ended up developing a pattern, of also, protecting the ones that hurt me... protecting him... protecting my parents... protecting your supposed friend... protecting you... and also protecting anyone that hurt me in my life... somehow I ended up protecting him as well... and I'm not going to protect them anymore... the ones that hurt me that is... including you...

So I'm telling you... You hurt me... and you hurt

me big time...

That supposed friend of yours... and I can't remember his name... that abused me as well...

I screamed and screamed for him to get off me... I screamed and screamed for him to get off me... and one of the things I remember about that particular time... was you... you... you... you sitting in the corner and watching... and watching your supposed friend... I screamed at you... my supposed relative 2... I screamed and screamed for your help too... and you didn't help... all you could do was watch... and smile... the more I screamed... the more you smiled... you smiled... and smiled more... at your little relative being abused... your little relative... a little relative of yours being abused... all you could do was smile... you couldn't do anything but smile... and your smile got bigger... the more I yelled for this to stop, stop, stop...

In that moment... my hate for you grew soooooooooo much... when the abuse was over... all I could do was scream at you... scream how much I hat-

I am closing that door

ed you... "You have no idea, how much I fucken hate you right now..." is what I screamed... In that moment I hated my relative 2, more than the abuser, who had abused me in that moment... Which is something, a little relative shouldn't have to feel for her bigger relative 2... I suppose you have no idea, what that did to me... My psyche had already had enough from my previous abuse ... from my Relative 1 who raped me... and from your sexual taunts...

> So I'm telling you... You hurt me... and you hurt me big time...

Then there was that time at a later stage... when I witnessed, what I witnessed... I can only describe it as... What must have been the aftermath of what you put my sister through in the bathroom... I know my psyche died that day... I happened to come across you and my little sister... anyways, I couldn't cope with what I saw... Not after what I had been through... I had come to the point, where my psyche could not handle this no longer... I felt I could not save anyone, any longer, in that moment... I had come *to a turning point within my psyche... I died within myself...so to speak... In that moment I crawled into the deepest, darkest place I could find...I felt I had dealt with more than I could possibly, humanly deal with, within that moment... I don't know how old I was... I could have been 12 maybe 13... I'm not sure... Way too young to have come to that point in my life... literally my psyche died that day... you don't know how many dark holes I have crawled out of since then...*

...So I'm telling you... You hurt me... and you hurt me big time...

This is how I recognise it...and I want you to recognise how I see it...

Your, Little Relative

Interestingly, after reading the Big Relative 2 letter to my Counsellor, she made a comment that when I read her the letter, which was to my Relative 1, it was a letter, which was written from, the child's point of view. The letter to my Big Relative 2 was definitely written from an adult's point of view, she said. This goes to show, as far as she was concerned, I had come a long way in my healing process.

I am closing that door

As my counsellor said, before I read my relative 2 letter. She said it could, go a few ways. He would perhaps recognize and admit wrong, he could totally deny or he could see it from a different point of view. I believe I witnessed, all those reactions from my relative 2, on the night I read him the letter. Not that he exactly admitted wrong. Initially he did say, he thought he was the only one, but then ended up talking, like it happened to all of us. The other thing he didn't do was apologise. As my counsellor reminded me, I don't have to rescue everybody, so put it behind me and move on, is exactly what I did.

To date, my relative 2 hasn't had anything to do with me. Even though, I now have a new phone number, and there is still my younger brother and sister (if they still want anything to do with him). But there would be others out there, that know my phone number and he could try and get in touch with me, via them and apologise, if he wanted to. So I am guessing, he has gone into and still is in the denial stage. I can live with that. I have lived with worse, much worse.

Paedophile and Protégé

Yesterday, 16/3/13, my little sister spoke to our big relative 2. My sister told my relative 2, that I read her that letter (Big Relative 2 letter) for her own healing process, before I left the country and that she was hoping to react to it, before I actually did leave the country, but never did. Better late, than never, I say. He said, "Ahh that letter" and then reckoned my letter was half full of lies. This comment tells me, he is still in the denial stage.

He did say to my sister, "I did try, feeling Lorne up". But she wouldn't let me; apparently I would always fight him off. I wonder if he realised that, I got perceptive and alert enough that I realised, this was my only defence, and I needed to shield or buffer myself from attack, as best as I could, whether he remembers or not, I must have had good reason to fight him off. I myself do have memories of always fighting him off, but it is a glint of a memory, of fighting him off. Always having to combat him off explains to me, why he got sly and sneaky in his approach to me.

I am referring to my memory of a bedroom incident in Ar-

I am closing that door

thur St, at this stage, my sister and I was sleeping in a single bed (while we were still waiting for our crates of furniture, etc. to arrive from England). I was the one on the outside of the bed, which was pushed against the wall. I do have that memory of being on the outside of the bed. I remember even though there was reluctance, a reluctance to be a victim of another sexual insult/taunt, I would be on the outside of the bed to protect my little sister.

I was still asleep, early hours of the morning, I woke up with having no blankets on and to him pulling at my knickers and touching my arse and sensing his fingers trying to move to vicinity, which is even more sacred to any girl. As soon as I realized what was happening, I remember swiping my arm/hand behind me, which was at him and told him, in no uncertain terms, to 'fuck off' – I still had to tell it, in a quiet nature, as I didn't want to wake up the rest of the household. I can't remember, if my hand or arm connected with him or not! I swiftly looked behind me and saw his face and remember that look on his face. He had by then, scooted back to the bedroom door, in his sly sneaky style. He had slunk back to the door, out of reach and before he whizzed, out of the bedroom, the smile on his face told me, ha-ha, I got away with that one. So perhaps my hand/arm didn't attach with him. I know there were other moments that he got away with it.

That sly sneaky style, I am talking about, means he was

poised for any possible action/reaction. It was recognizable, he had pre-planned it and was prepared for any fast, quick action that he had to take. He knew what he was doing and he prepared himself for a quick withdrawal from the room, just in case. He was anticipating the worse, as he knew there could be worse. That is why he did it in the crafty, devious style he did as he was used to it. I remember often going to bed and having that feeling, of having to be 'on guard' (another pattern created, because of my Relative 1 and my big relative 2 imbedded it even further). I know there were nights, I went to bed not wanting to fall asleep, not knowing what to expect and not knowing when the next incident might happen. All because of his shrewd and shifty, approach to me.

Our big relative 2 apologised to my sister, he admitted to her he was a bully or tyrant and admitted to the offences he did to my sister in the bathroom. He admitted what he did to my sister was traumatic for her. My sister told him how I had internalised everything and consequently, was a very sick person for many years, that knowledge didn't even budge his thoughts, re apologising to me.

Big relative 2 said, the Special School he used to go to, used to hypnotise him as part of their therapy for dyslexia and they also gave him counselling. He suggested the hypnotism may have blanked his memories as he was surprised at some of what, my little sister was saying about her memories. It is my suggestion here, that not necessarily did the hypnotism block some of his memory. It could have been that he blocked his memory naturally, just like his little relatives' did.

Big relative 2 told my sister, he remembers Nan n Grandads' Butcher Shop. When they had the Butcher Shop, he used to go to there, after school. He said, that when Bert got there, on a Thursday after work, Bert used to take him to the bathroom and show our big relative 2, black n white photographs of girls 'sucking his (Bert's) dick'. It got to the stage he reckoned, Bert would take him to the bathroom and used to masturbate in front him and encouraged my relative 2 to do the same to himself. He tells my sister, he refused to do the same. I am going to say here, we don't know what he may have blocked from his memory. Perhaps big relative 2 has blocked out, being touched by Bert, re masturbation. He has the memories of being told, "You grab one and I will grab the other…"

He tells my sister that, he remembers the bunks in the boys' room, getting us girls onto either bunk. He remembers Bert telling him "You grab one and I'll grab the other…" Big relative 2 reckons he remembers, never doing this to me. He reckoned I would not let him. Of course, I wouldn't let him, I would combat him off. I was the bigger sister and my little sister was easier, for him to grab, Relative 1 Bert was the one that always grabbed me.

Big relative 2 tells my sister that on another day, Bert got my sister naked, laid her on the bed and said to my big relative 2 "Go for it, you can fuck her…" Does he have the memory of what happened before/after that? Even though, this is my big relative 2's memory, I have to ask here, with as many memories that we have blocked out. Had Bert done the same to me, that particular day? Had Bert laid me naked on a bed and fucked me, before he undressed my little sister and suggested to my big relative 2, "Go for it, you can fuck her…" It is a known fact that is how a person, who is grooming his protégé, would work. Show them how it is done first and then tell them to go ahead.

The memory of me and Tokoroa Entity was big relative 2 playing Relative 1 Bert, the Paedophile. My big relative 2 was watching, gleefully as his 'friend' was violating me.

My big relative 2 was Bert's Protégé. Bert trained my big relative 2 into being the Paedophile. Putting these labels, Protégé, Paedophile, on either my Relative 1 or relative 2, has really only just occurred to me. I know what they did. I know that my sister and I suffered shockingly and appallingly as children, but those labels. I have only just thought of it in this light, since talking to my sister, the other day. But that is exactly, what was happening in England. My Relative 1, the Paedophile, was prepping my big relative 2, as his Protégé.

How many other Protégés did Bert train? That is a scary thought.

Who taught Bert? How many Protégés, did that particular person have? Some more scary thoughts. The questions can go on and on, along this line.

Bert was a grown man when he did this to us. He should have known better! He should have been protecting us. He should have been protecting all of us. But he did it anyway!

By the time that Tokoroa Entity incident happened and the incident mentioned just below, my relative 2 was old enough, to know better as well!

At this stage big relative 2 will not apologise to me for anything else, as he said to my sister, he feels he never did anything to me. But apparently big relative 2 is now contemplating apologising to me, if only for the trauma he put through, re me seeing him and my sister in bathroom scene. This is referred to in the big relative 2 letter. The day my sister begged and pleaded with our parents not to go out, but they did go out. The day she tells me, he (big relative 2) got her clothes off and tried to fuck her, she did her best, not to let him enter her and she succeeded.

This is not it, for my sister, she tells me. She hasn't given up, wanting to talk to our big relative 2 more. She tells me, she is still going to talk to relative 2, further re contemplation of apologizing to me. She feels strongly that big relative 2 should apologise to me as well, even though he had blocked memories from his own past. I haven't heard from him, to this day (27.5.14).

Another one of big relative 2's memories that he told my sister, is getting my little sister and her friend into a bedroom and getting the girls to scream. He is standing against the door, inside the room, forcing it shut, so I couldn't get in. I was trying to struggle and push from the other side, to see what the girls were screaming about. He was using all his force, so I couldn't get in that room.

I have to ask. Why, why did he do that? Was that his way, of trying to get to me on a psychological level, to torment me into thinking, he was doing something to both of the girls in that room? I bet he had a big grin on his face that time as well. As I am typing this, I am actually getting memories of slamming my fist against a door and just giving up in pure hindrance and defeat, as I can't get in. Was that, that occasion or was that another occasion. I am not sure! Or did he wait for me to give up and then do whatever to the girls. Maybe, maybe not, as my sister did have her friend with her. Going by the memory of my younger brother (mentioned further along in this book), not tolerating me into that room, was big relative 2 being Bert's Protégé as well.

I am closing that door

My sister also told big relative 2, it was our intention to say something to Relative 1 Bert, when we visited England – to have Bert up, with what he did to us, as children. But seeing him suffering big time and accepting the fact that, karma had caught up with him. We thought that was enough, we thought we were contented at the time, as he was suffering big time.

"Funny you should mention that", said big relative 2, he was going to do that, when he was in England (1995). He went to Nan's place, knowing Bert would be there on this day. When Bert got there, after his days' work, Bert said matter-of-factly "Ahh what are you doing here!" Not for instance: OMG, arms stretched out, to greet a relative, which he hadn't seen for many years. But big relative 2 didn't have the courage to say anything about the horrific past, just like us, as Bert had two young children and a marriage. As I have discovered, there is the right time for everything in life, including the right time to have someone up about how they created such a horrific, stressful life for us.

As it has turned out, for me, more and more memories have resurfaced, as time has gone by, since last seeing Bert. Because of all the healing processes I have been through and the accumulative memories from my sister and big relative 2 (via my sister), I now have more to say within this book, so to speak. If this book was to turn up

Lorne Driscoll

at Bert's house, there is now way more here within this book, than any of us, as an individual would be able to say in person, back then.

Big relative 2 told me, re was going to tell Bert while in England, when I read him this letter to him (relative 2 letter). As I have said previously, he thought he was the only one and later on, he was talking like it occurred to all of us. He also said that same evening that he doesn't remember the supposed friend incident and that mum wouldn't allow friends home, after school. If he remembers or not, in this case he must have gone behind her back, as he did take this friend home after school and this so called friend did violate me, I know, I am the one that it happened to. I am the one that this supposed friend violated.

I am grateful for my sister taking the time and telling big relative 2, what she thought, as some of what he told her, is actually helping me, piece together some of the puzzle from my past and no doubt, it would be the same for her. I hope she pursues talking to him more, if she can, if only for her own healing process.

We children, more so, we 3 older children all have our own memories, as to what happened to us, when we were growing up. Some of these memories are different and some actually get to the stage where they sort of interlink. I am sure, if we were adult enough, to all get together

I am closing that door

and actually put some time aside and just talked about our memories of our horrific abusive childhood. I am sure that would, open up the pathway to actually interlink some of these memories together and perhaps allow other memories to come forth and put more of the puzzle together, for all of us. I know my sister and I could do this (and have done this in the past) and I know my younger brother, even though he said, he has no memories of this, I am sure he has just blocked out, what he must have heard. If he was to get together with me and my sister even, maybe hearing us talk about our memories, maybe that would start to jog some memory for him and in turn, for us. As for big relative 2, he is going through the denial stage (with me) so that wouldn't be possible for all 4 of us to get together, until we were all ready. I remember my younger brother, telling me a memory, which was jogged for him while I read him the Big Relative 2 letter. I read it to him for his healing purpose, as well as my own.

He told me, he remembers that you 3 (older kids) were shut in a room with Bert and he (younger brother) was shut out of the room and told not to go in, as much as, at the time he really did want to go into that room. He kept asking to go into that room, because at the time he thought he was 'missing out on the fun'. Eventually, giving up, as he was told no every time. He now realises, since I read him that letter, maybe it wasn't fun after all.

I actually have my own memory of being inside that room (our girls' bedroom) that my younger brother was trying to get into. I remember standing there and just willing my young brother not to be so persistent and to give up asking. I remember being imposed to stay in that room, I remember being told to be silent and not say a word. I remember being frightened and scared out of my wits, not knowing what was going to happen next. I knew it was not good for my younger brother, to be on the same side of the door as we were. I do wonder if my young brother's memory is that occasion or another one.

8/9/11 (10/11/10 was my 1st session)

Make sure I'm not rescuing my next relationship

Guide – look at what I want in a relationship

The characteristics that I want – personality – see how they treat their mum. This will be a tell-tale sign, on how they will treat you, she tells me.

Respect

Kindness

Accepting each other for each other

It's not all about the sex appeal

I am closing that door

What's in the heart of a man? This is important.

Pleased that I have come a long way. I went through leaps and bounds going through this process of being counselled.

Always remember that it is not my fault

Don't take on board, if there is a step back → when giving letter to relative 2, or any process of the healing journey.

Burn or send or tear it up Relative 1 letter. Now included in this book, as well as posted with a mock address on it.

Get a new start, a new telephone number, to break that connection → stop at the top of the Brynderwyns' → send him a text → then put new sim card in.

Last Visit

Last visit with H.... 28/9/11

*Make an osteopath ap*pointment. Looking after me is important.

I'm actually looking after me...

I have got to do this for me...

For the first time in my life, I'm focusing on what is good for me...

This is not about hurting you, it's about me...

I've sacrificed myself long enough, way too long.

I'm not going to do it anymore... I am not going to sacrifice myself any longer.

At the ripe old age of 50, I'm turning a new leaf in my book...this leaf is all about me

I am closing that door

I have to do what is right for me… I have to do what is right for me.

You have possibly realised, by reading my notes that not only was I being counselled for what happened to me in my past. I was also being counselled, with what I was going through, with my partner at the time. This also happened to be related, with what I went through as a child, my partner at the time, was a reflection of what I went through as a child. He tapped into the trauma of the unrecognized abused, wounded and terrified child. He reflected all the negativity and other raw, indescribable emotions that I experienced as a child and had been through; to that stage I am sure.

The unnamed ex-partner will immediately know who he is, if he ever reads this book. He might even identify perhaps, certain things I have mentioned in this book, if he remembers what little I told him, when I was trying to talk to him about my past. He told me, he memorised the letter I wrote, re reasons, why I need to leave him, that I believe of him and that I know he did.

I want to take this opportunity to thank you, as you were a portion of the reason, why I come to be on this path of writing this book. I think you now know that I needed to do this by myself, so I can move forward with my life.

I hope you have moved on with your life. I hope you have found someone else, I also truly hope that you have become a better person, because if you haven't, whoever she is, if she has any sense, will leave you as well.

Letter to Tokoroa Entity

10/3/13

Below is the letter, I attempted to write to Tokoroa Entity. I wrote this letter roughly at the time and maybe before, I was writing the letters to Relative 1 Bert and Big Relative 2. I couldn't finish the letter at the time. My emotions and/or reactions were extremely high and turbulent during that period and my writing was becoming very changeable. I saved the actual letter on refill, as I knew there would come the point that I would attempt to finish this letter. Maybe, I just need to add it, as is, as I have overcome so much since then. Once I have written it in the Counselling notes, as I will write it as I wrote it back then, I will get great gratification in tearing the refill version up, into little pieces.

Tokoroa Entity

I remember you were my relative 2's so-called 'friend'

I remember your skin colour, you were brown

I remember you were stocky-ish in build

I remember you were roughly my relative 2's age at the time

Whatever your name is, I can't remember, but I remember you...

I'm not going to let you rule my life anymore, as I remember what you did as well

I remember you violated me

I remember the smirk → I remember the smirk from my relative 2 and you

I remember telling my relative 2 in no uncertain terms, how much I hated him and I am so glad I did...

I'm so glad I told my relative 2, how much I hated him... n that I did...

How much I hated him and you in that moment...

The thing is I directed that hate more at him,

I am closing that door

than I did you, in the moment → but I also meant to say it to you as well… I hated you as well in that moment…in that moment…

I can only remember (you doing it) once, but once is more than enough; my memory has blocked it, if there were more occasions

I'm not going to let you rule my life anymore

Do you know why I am glad now, as much as I hated you in that moment, because that is as far as I remember, the last time it happened to me…

The unfortunate thing is, I now know, it could very well be the time, when my big relative 2 picked on my little sister… but I was glad, I'm not the one (being picked on) anymore…

But you don't realise how you affected my life, because I was put in the position of not being able to save my little sister

Do you know how much that screwed up my head?

When I saw what I saw

Lorne Driscoll

You are not going to rule my life anymore.

I found rewriting this letter into the counselling notes and typing it, into this book, easier than I ever thought it would be. When I first wrote the above letter on refill, it was soooo hard. The emotions I felt, at the time while writing it, was so enormously intense. I remember the anger was the strongest emotion at the time, but the other emotions, which were mixed up with that anger, were inexpressible. I thought at the time, it should be the easiest letter to write, as basically, this is the one with the name I can't remember. Maybe that is why; it was the hardest to write at the time, because I couldn't remember the name. Or it could have been the hardest at the time, as it was the lead up to, not be able to save my sister the last time. The reason why, doesn't matter anymore, the fact that I have let go off so much is the important thing. It does go to show over time, how things can change. I have gotten over so much, just by letting go off so much.

I was right, as I was writing the Tokoroa Entity letter into my book, more of his facial appearances, became clearer in my mind. I am now beginning to think, if I was to see a picture of him, as he was back then, I am pretty sure I could point him out.

As I said in this letter to the Tokoroa Entity, I only remember him doing it once, if there were other occasions, that he abused me, my memory has blocked it out. I do have that memory that, if this 'friend' was around after school, that I was safer in my bedroom, rather than in the lounge, where those boys were. I now know the above letter is sufficient to let the Tokoroa Entity know, what he did and how it affected me and the above letter will let him know how I see it, if he ever reads this book. I now know the rest of the book will explain it even further. Not just explain it further to him, but also the book will explain it further to the other abusers in my life.

Immeasurable Emotions

Luckily, I was home alone this particular night as well. The emotions, anger I felt and crying I did this night was immeasurable, again. Even though I didn't add these notes to my counselling notes, I remembered my Counsellors words and wrote them on scrap paper, which was the only thing I had available in the moment. I needed to vent this unsettled turmoil that I was experiencing this night, hence the same red type. I wanted to add these words as they were in the moment, just like my counselling notes.

Aired 13.5.13 on a programme called 'A Current Affair' (Channel 9), brought me to tears, so much so, I didn't hear some of what she said, but in the moment, everything she said, made sense, if that makes sense. *Re Rolf Harris* and her encounter of *sex abuse, that he put her through. I think her name might have been Tonya Leigh (not sure of spelling).* I have since found that her name is spelt Tonya Lee. Tonya, I wish to thank you for your bravery for coming forward and speaking your truth. I hope you give others the

I am closing that door

strength to come forward, as you were not only healing yourself, by doing this interview. I know you were healing for me as I heard you speak. I know more than likely, you were healing for others that may have heard you.

What might have been a slight incident to him, no matter how many times, he may have done it to her or anyone else – he has no idea the impact that has had on the rest of her/their life.

My life as a child was horrifyingly horrific, not just one incident, but many – I had no way of dealing with it – it was way easier to bury. The impact that had on my life was tremendously frightening beyond words.

If that one impact had, had that much effect on her life… Even though I already was aware the impact my abuse had, had on my life. Someway, somehow, hearing what she said, helped me put into perspective the many times I was violated, how that had a tremendous impact on my life and just how mind-blowing and devastating that abuse was on my life.

Relative 1 Bert/Big Relative 2/Tokoroa Entity, you have no idea how much what you did to me/us… that impacted our life beyond words.

Lorne Driscoll

FUCK I HATE YOU.... FUCK I didn't know how much emotion was still wrapped up in this...

This night not only did I hate the violators in my life, but I hated her violator and even hated the celebrity mentioned below, who had a mention in this news clip and other news clips.

Hearing her speak explains to me, that's probably why I was chubby at the age of 13, I could relate to her use of comfort food and went down to a size of 7 stone at the age of 13/14. I had, had major surgery at the time and afterwards, I was 7 to 7 ½ stone for a long time. I could relate to her saying, she couldn't eat at times.

How could I have let them be favourite celebrities' way back then especially Jimmy Savile he seemed to be cool way back then, when I was growing up...

13.5.13. I was so angry with myself this night for allowing myself to think they were so cool, not just angry but insurmountable, indescribable other emotions, I cannot even begin to explain, especially how much I hate those celebrities right now. I know that this anger and overwhelming indescrib-

I am closing that door

able emotion was also aimed at the abusers in my life.

In my opinion the abuser generally, has no idea that could even be the case, as they are too busy getting their own self-gratification. Generally, it wouldn't dawn on them, to realise that the abusee is going through these extremely mixed emotions and feelings, and rightly so they are going through these emotions and feelings. Consequently having these extremities impact the abusee life to one extreme or the other. In a lot of cases the abusee life is impacted for the rest of that abusee life. I was so angry about this on this night. At least I had released my feelings in the form of writing it down and crying it out.

Here I will add a notation I wrote a year later, but will still keep it in the same red type, as it was written in the moment.

16.5.14

Feeling anguish, frustration and the unknowing.

Don't know why, but just feeling frustration

Just need to breathe it out

Anger is coming in there as well...

Just need to breathe it out

Breathe it out…

It is good to write this as it is helping in making me feel better

And the messy scribble overleaf I did was a big letting go

Work Secret

When I moved to Australia I attained a full time job, not long after being here. On practically day one of my new job, my daughter and I were asked to keep a secret. She was about to go back to work on a part-time basis, with the same company. We were told that the company did not like family members working together. I felt I was pretty lucky to get a job, so soon after arriving in Australia and I certainly didn't want to jeopardise my daughter's opportunity to earn some money for her family. I know that she didn't want jeopardise my chances, on my new job, in a new country and a new life. So keeping the secret we did. I didn't mind keeping this secret as I wanted myself and my daughter to keep our jobs. Over the cause of time, it was easy to keep this secret, especially while she was working on a part-time basis (1 day a week). However the other family connections, that were eventually emerging at work, was becoming hypocritical of the companies supposed stand with us, nonetheless we still kept our secret.

About a year later my daughter went back to full time work with the same company. By that stage, hardly anyone knew this secret, except her interviewer and HR personal at head office and a selected few, for one reason or the other became part of the secret. The interviewer, which interviewed me and eventually became the Operations Manager, I might be wrong, but I am sure he still has no idea, to date (8.6.13) that we are mum and daughter.

It got to the stage that some of the colleagues sitting in my daughters' pod worked it out, that we were mum and daughter, but our relationship was still low key. I then eventually, told one of my colleagues in my pod, feeling happy and relieved that I had told her and left it at that, for a while.

My daughter and I decided, I should tell a few of the others in my pod, after we were seen talking together one day. I remember when I told these two colleagues on this day, just by telling them and letting it go, just how liberating it was. It wasn't until one of them mentioned how good I am in keeping secrets. I thought to myself, yes, I was trained at a very early age into keeping secrets. No wonder I am good at keeping secrets now. But those childhood secrets, I was trained into keeping, were secrets you shouldn't be forced into keeping. It was harmful and destructive in being forced to keeping that type secret. The work secret, as hypocritical as it seemed at times – we were saving our jobs and if we wanted to keep our relationship secret, that was up to us. It was our choice to be secret about it or not.

I am closing that door

But the childhood secrets that I was forced to keep when I was a child were being destructive to mind, body and soul. Those secrets should not be kept, as they are destructive and caustic, very destructive and caustic.

I am now glad, that I had that opportunity, to experience that feeling of liberation, in telling this work secret. As I am now, beginning to think that the redeeming feeling that I experienced when I told the two colleagues, will be a stepping stone for the freedom I will feel, when this book is published. But I feel the liberation I will feel will be immeasurable, compared to what I felt on the day, I told these two colleagues.

I am now, so looking forward to having this book published.

I am so looking forward to having that feeling of liberation.

Letter to All 3 of Them

As an addition to the letters that I have written to my violators and added to this book – below I have written a letter, to all 3 of you together.

If the 3 of you don't know who you are, it wouldn't take much for you or anyone else to work out who you are. Even Tokoroa Entity, I am sure you know who you are, if you read this book. Even though I don't remember your actual name, with today's technology, it's just a bit harder for someone else to work out your identity, is all.

I am not just any Jane Smith writing this book. My name is not only unique, but my name is extremely unique and I have penned my real name to this book.

Once this book is published, it is beyond my control what happens thereafter, and that is a fact.

I am closing that door

Here is the letter to all 3 of you:

To Relative 1 Bert/Big Relative 2/Tokoroa Entity

The depths of the soul can become destroyed. It can get crushed, crushed and crushed again. Keeping what you did to me silent, is letting you, all of you, get away with the horrors you put me through.

You are NOT having me anymore. I have taken me back. I have taken Lorne back. I am *Braving the Unknown* by publishing this book.

You can't crush or destroy me anymore. My Soul is free, from all of you.

I just gave my Inner Child the voice she needed and told it, like it was. We will *brave the unknown* together; therefore I am letting my Inner Child have her freedom, by voicing this in the form of this book.

The 5 year old in me, is now free from all of you. I am now even going to say 4 year old and perhaps even younger, as I feel the abuse even happened before I turned 5. I am saying that, as I was already in the habit of saving and protecting at 5 years of age.

The 4 year old in me

The 5 year old in me

The 6 year old in me

The 7 year old in me

The 8 year old in me

The 9 year old in me

The 10 year old in me

The 11 year old in me

The 12 year old in me

The 13 year old in me…

The young pre-schooler, the young girl, within all those ages mentioned above, who is called Lorne and the adult woman Lorne, who is writing this book, are now all free from all of you.

I will have my freedom and have this book out there, one way of the other.

Lorne

Letter to the Readers

To the readers of this book:

The truth needs to be out there, this book is my truth and I am putting my truth out there, to be known, to be read and to be heard.

From a personal prospective, the purpose of writing this book is to tell the truth and give my Inner Child the voice she needs. Giving us the healing process we need. Letting go off a horrific past and consequently, not only breaking a cycle on an unconscious level, that has been happening for centuries but also is allowing for a much better future and peace of mind – and peace of mind is precious. I am writing this book, for my own emotional, physical and spiritual well-being. I hope by reading this book that it is a healing process, for someone out there, anyone out there. I also hope that parents especially, became aware that this could happen unknowingly to them. These are the reasons, why I am writing this book and for no other reason.

Both my sister and I, brought our children up, to say it is ok to tell someone, about it and it's ok to say no. Two books that I read to my children were (I also encouraged them to ask any questions they might have), 'What's Wrong with Bottoms?' by Jenny Hessell and 'We Can Say No!' by David Pithers and Sarah Greene. I encourage any parent out there to read these types of books to their children, but try not to make them fearful at the same time. There would be numerous titles, especially now with the Internet, that is available, that would be appropriate to encourage your child, with confidence to say no, if necessary. This would be preparing your child or children, at an appropriate age, with a Child's Guide in protecting them from dangerous people. You never know if it might be needed.

From another personal perspective talking about letting go, I have had a long history of sicknesses and surgeries. I believe, the sicknesses and a lot of those surgeries especially, were a consequence of internalising what I went through and *keeping silent*. *Keeping silent* and internalising what happened was extremely stressful, and very destructive on my body. However, with the journey of writing this book, the numerous chest/throat infections I have had over the past two years especially, I believe are a letting go process. That is my body's way of ejecting all those horrible toxins within my body. Those were the horrible toxins and negativities, which my body has hung onto all this time, as I *kept silent*. These toxins are finally being eliminated from my body and soul. I am now willing, to tell it like it was, as I want to let go of my horrific past, for my emotional, physical and spiritual well-being.

I can tell you that writing this book has been very healing and therapeutic. The raw emotions that I have experienced have been immense at times while writing this book. I put myself so close to my childhood by writing about it, I am now beginning to recognise more of those habitual thoughts I had way back then, as they resurfaced or became more recognisable as habitual thoughts (regardless of how long it took me to recognise that), while I was going back to my childhood. Now I am recognising the fact that these habitual thoughts did resurface, as I was writing this book, even with sometimes not recognising that it was happening at times or in the moment. Now I do recognise them, there will be more habitual thoughts that I can let go off. I also know, the closer I am getting this book to the stage where I can send this book to my Proof Reader, before it goes to the Publisher, I know that there is raw emotion still sitting there, just waiting to come out. I know that as, unwittingly I have cried at the drop of a hat, just lately… I know, when I send this book to my Proof Reader/Publisher, I know I will cry. As it turns out, I cried and cried on the day leading up to passing this on to my Proof Reader. When this book is actually published I will tear my counselling notes up into little pieces and burn all the little pieces (if I have somewhere to do so, safely at the time). That will be yet, another letting go.

I hope someone else out there can do the same. I hope I can give someone, who has been through or going through abuse, the courage to *brave the unknown* and tell it like it was/is.

Whether you write it in book form like me, or just write it in letter form and give it to the abuser anonymously or in person. Or write it in letter form and just tear the letter up or burn the letter (it goes without saying, in a safe manner, of course☺). Or just tell the person concerned in person, if you feel you can. Or perhaps, try the message in the bottle, into the sea thing, so you have that actual, physically letting go off the past.

It is up to you, how you do it, even if you draw/pen your feelings out or just talk to a confidante. No matter, how small or big a step you take, it will be a process of letting go and it will be the healing process you deserve. Please do not suffer in silence.

As keeping the abuse silent, is allowing them to get away with the abuse.

Lorne

The Impact of Writing This Book

As an addition to this book, I am going to let the reader know that the Impact of writing this book has had more effect on me than I ever realised it would. This chapter will give me the opportunity to mention the good things that have come out of this journey in writing this book and indicate why I have put off sending this book to the Publisher.

Considering the contents of this book, I actually enjoyed writing this book, as it was a new found way for me to release my emotions in a creative way. As mentioned before, putting me so close to my childhood by writing about it is the thing that I didn't like, sometimes more than others. I didn't like it as it brought up the same feelings and emotions that I experienced in my childhood, it put me in a very vulnerable state. The same or similar state I was, as a terrified abused and frightened young girl. At the same time I knew that this was all to do with the healing process of letting go. The impact of thinking this book was finished and ready to go to a Publisher scared me. So much so, that I actually put off sending this book to a Publisher. I decided to write this book in 2011, I started actually writing in mid to late 2012, but I kind of put it aside, even after my Proof Reader went over this mid-2013. He even said you could send it to the Publisher as is, if you wanted to, as it is the truth and that is what people want to read... I still hung onto it (yes, I did add more, critiqued and critiqued more after the Proof Reader had it). There was a part of me that couldn't let this go, as I was scared.

I started this Chapter on 29.4.14, after adding a few bits to the body of the book a few days before. Then I started adding more to the body of the book after that date. This was after several months of not adding any more to this book. On 7.4.14, I visited an Osteopath for the first time since being in Australia. After suggesting I seriously give myself some TLC, he then told me that hanging onto this book is actually killing me and he strongly suggested that I put a time line on this and let go off this book. If it is finished all well and good, if it is not finished, still let go off this. It is important that I let go for my own health, he was indicating. It is important to do it in the time frame that you nominate he said. You can always revisit this in say 5 years' time for instance and do a re-edition, if you wished, he added. His words have actually scared me back into action, I didn't realise it was having that type of huge impact on me on my life, full stop. Luckily I now have the time to work on this, as I was recently made redundant from my job. I am taking this redundancy as a blessing in disguise, as I need this time, to do just that and let go off this book. To help me let go off this book, still means that I am still going through more Self Improvement.

The time frame with the two dates mentioned in the above paragraph, is the time frame that I have spent on myself, as I was working such long hours and as I had put myself so close to my childhood, therefore putting me in a vulnerable stage, which had an effect on my work environment, my time there was becoming very stressful. I have needed to spend that time on me, as working those long hours was not good for me, under those circumstances. I also started writing this book, while working those long hours those at work. Heeding my Osteopath's words, I am now focusing on putting 4-5 hours aside a day for the time factor that I nominate, now I have the time, and then look for work that is more conducive to my needs. Letting go off this is exactly what I will do, during the time that I nominate, before I work full time in, finding the job that is better suited to me.

The biggest emotion that held me back in letting go off this book is fear. That is fear of rejection, fear of failure, fear of not being heard and many other fears, in amongst this fear was anger and resentment all planted in me, when I was a young girl. All that negative emotion had grown into bulging vines within me, adding to it are the relationships that I found myself in and have I endured into my adulthood.

The below is something I started typing separately to this book. It was after my visit to the Osteopath, it was thoughts on my mind at the time. I have now decided to include this in my book now, as it is just as crucial to this process as the rest of the book. It is still thoughts that I had, to do with what I am going through and that I was feeling in the moment. I will put this is in the same red type, as my Counselling notes that I took, even though they are from a different period. It will be good for these notes to stand out as well.

This is my book

This is my book. This is what I intend to let go off. What I have been through has been one of the biggest torments of my whole life. I have experienced anguish and all sorts of emotions and pain to the extreme. Now is the time to let go. This is one of my biggest fears to let go off, but I need to, if I hold on to this book – this will kill me. I choose to let go, so it doesn't kill me. I choose to let go so I can be there for my nearest and dearest. I choose to let go, so I can live a fuller life, a more peaceful life and I want to live life without

I am closing that door

this big huge shadow/cloud over me, destroying my insides. I feel I need to remind the readers here, this is my journey. Someone else could have a similar journey to me and say if they did go down the same path as me; their reaction could be different to what I went through. We are all different. We all react differently to each other, no matter what the situation.

During my childhood, I hated it every time that Relative 1 was there but then again I remember for some reason at times, I liked him being there (I am told this is normal reaction for someone that has been abused. One thing Relative 1 did have, he did have a sense humour, and he had a way of making people laugh around him. I suppose that was a disguise for his hideous intent) but that was because I never knew any different. I never understood why, until I became an adult. This is what I was used to, this is what I came to expect. This is what I knew. This is what I came to know as normal. I knew no different. I knew this as normal. My emotions were very mixed. My angst was huge. My mind was very crazy at times, but I couldn't put those words to that feeling or any feeling in the moment, being so young. This is what I knew, this is what I expected, knowing no different. As much as I knew

Lorne Driscoll

my Relative 1 shouldn't be doing what he was doing. I couldn't tell him to stop, he wouldn't listen to me saying stop. Being so young he over powered me, he over powered those that he should have protected.

There was a time where as an adult I had to ask myself, how he could do such a horrible thing to us? I was not the only one. Other questions I have asked myself over the time:

How could he be so disconnected with his humanness that he had to interfere with such young child/ren?

These children were his extended family. He interfered with his relative's children, how could he have done that?

I will perhaps never get answers to the above questions. Now I have come this far in my journey, I have now come to sort of understanding, but I am still not of a full understanding of the total implications of the karmic experience that is going on for all involved. Maybe I will never get that full understanding and if that is the case, that is OK. Maybe I am not meant to get a full understanding. Just understanding my karmic journey will be enough in this. I have been on a huge journey of healing and spiritual improvement that I am still wondering where the end is, but I think it close. I know that if I don't let go off this book, it will kill me and I don't want to take that chance, I have too much to live for.

As I said earlier in my book, I am not going to sweep under the carpet, the horrendous abuse that was inflicted upon us anymore. If I am meant to be part of a collective energy that is breaking a cycle, then that is what I am going to do. If that means I have to publish this book before this cycle actually breaks on the level that is intended, then that is exactly what I am going to do. This is my story.

It was suggested late last year (Nov 2013) that I write my own personal chapter, a chapter that is separate to the book. A chapter that I could vent, whatever emotions into this chapter that I wanted to, vent the core of my soul if I wanted to. You don't need to include this, if you don't want to, was the suggestion. These questions below are just as vital to anyone that has gone through this. Questions that just as likely would be on the mind of any abusee. These are questions that generally go unheard, so therefore I have decided to include this piece of the chapter below, also in red type.

My Personal Chapter for Me

This is a chapter for me — and no one else to see. This is to allow me to vent, whatever emotions into this chapter that I would like. If I decide, to allow anyone to see this, that is up to me.

This is to do with my childhood and therefore this is also to allow my Inner Child to vent anything she would like. Right now this seems to be in the form of unanswered questions.

Why weren't you there for me?

Why didn't you see?

Why did you not guess? Were there any tell-tale signs that your children were being violated?

Why did you not stop it?

How come it had to happen so many times?

Did you know how much I how hated it?

Did you know that it affected my life in an un-

I am closing that door

imaginable way, even into adulthood?

Did you know it robbed me of way more than one could even imagine?

Didn't you see the anguish, the grief, the pain, the moments when things were not OK?

Didn't you wonder in the slightest, what was going on?

Couldn't you see I was screaming on the inside?

Why, why, why, why me? Why did you do this to me?

Why did you do this to us?

I felt so angry, I felt so angry, so angry. I felt all these different emotions and I didn't know how to deal with these emotions. I felt these emotions could not be expressed by someone so young and could not be understood by someone so young.

The above questions are the many questions not only, some of which I wanted to ask my perpetrators. But mostly these are questions that I have wanted to ask my parents and/or any adult *that should have had answers to those questions, even if it was just some of those questions. These are questions that I will not necessarily get answers to anymore and some of them will always remain, just that, questions. These questions that remain unanswered have slowly become less urgent to answer. I realise it is OK to have unanswered questions. Hanging onto these unanswered questions, could eat you up, consume you, and be destructive on the inside. I am so glad that I got to break the cycle. I am so glad, I am dealing with this and glad my book will help others out there. I want this book to reach the multitude out there, that need this.*

After a life time of bringing up two children in NZ, I eventually followed my heart and moved to Australia, I arrived with two big suitcases and two cardboard boxes. On my arrival my son-in-law unpacked the car and suggested that I travelled heavy. Yes the suitcases were heavy but I said to him "you realise that is my life you are carrying in there". When I spoke those words out loudly, I realised the freedom I felt, for moving so lightly. I gave most of my possessions away and what little I sold, I sold them really cheaply, before leaving NZ. I have realised on hindsight that, that de-cluttering in my life in NZ, was all in prepa-

I am closing that door

ration of the massive letting go, that I am about to let go off, in this book. This has been such a mammoth journey.

As mentioned before there are many healers I have been to in the past. I am so pleased I went to see them and thank you, to you all. Big thanks also go, to the most sincere, the most non-judgemental person I have ever come across and she such a beautiful lady, from the Breathing School that I am seeing at this time. By creating such a safe haven, she has helped me to breathe out those fears that I hung to. The fears that were created because of the abuse I suffered. I know the resentment has gone and we are working on the anger. She has helped me with so much and I have let go off so much emotionally, since I have been seeing her. I was able to let go off the blood curdling scream, which I should have let go off, when I was 12 or 13 and I have been able to shed an old identity. By the time my time restriction is up, to get this book to the Publisher, I am sure that most of that anger will be gone, if not nearly. I still do have on the occasion, agitated reactions to certain news clips in the media, when it comes to this subject. Those triggered moments are becoming lesser and lesser. I do have and will book another appointment before that time period is up. The Osteopath I have been seeing since I have been in Australia, actually go hand in hand for me, because, as I breathe out these emotions and the body adjusts to the consequential change, my Osteopath will gently manipulate and realign my body accordingly or as he sees fit. I am so grateful for his time in my self-improvement.

As mentioned earlier in this book, the imprint of this abuse is still there, that will never leave me. But living with the imprint, is much better than living with those negative emotions attacking my insides, this is much better than having those triggers affect me, the way they used to. Last night (12.6.14) I had a happy memory return. The memory of us sitting in front of an open fire and our dad was telling us stories. Pretending the sparks clinging to the side of the fire place were soldiers. My dad was a fantastic story teller and we would listen with intent as he told his stories. I thought I would mention this as this is a happy memory that had been buried for a long time and has resurfaced. It is good I am remembering this happy memory.

This whole process of going through these healing procedures and journey of writing this book is helping to make Lorne, a new Lorne. I am a different woman since the beginning of writing this book. A different woman, which is now for the better and it is, all a positive step for a better life. Creating this book has not only given me strength to help others in their journey of healing, in ways I was never able to help others before. Writing this book has also given me the opportunity to let go off many, many emotions that I have held onto since childhood, emotions and feelings that held me captive in my past with old patterns that

I am closing that door

I was repeating. I have infinite thanks and beyond for this opportunity to let go off those old patterns that have held me captive to my past. I have immense thanks for the opportunity of writing this book. I also have an untold thanks to all of those that have helped and encouraged me along the way. I am still getting used to the new me actually, but I can tell you I have become much healthier and stronger, emotionally, spiritually and physically. I also know that I have a continuing path of Self Improvement, so more of me to discover. It does sound exciting.

I am looking forward to what happens, once I do let go off this book. I am imagining that my life will still change for the better and keep changing for the better. Now I have found this new way of creative expression within me, more than likely, I will go on write another book, once this one is out there. If I do go ahead and write another book, it maybe a completely different topic. I am looking forward to seeing whatever it is, that will happen.

It is important to me that this book gets out there and I *now* have faith and trust my book is successful in helping not just one person but more people that I thought possible, in their journey. I know that writing this book and the interaction with my support people has helped in healing my past and therefore has healed me in the now. The core changes within me have given me way more confidence to let go off this book. I have now let go off the hold that this book has on me. Being able to let go off the hold this book has had over me is my saving grace.

Now as I let go off this book, now as I let go off these pages within this book and release them to the universe, I release them with healing thoughts. I send this book out there to the universe to all those that need to read it. This book is sent with love, compassion, empathy, peace, faith and trust to heal those that need it. Now I let go off this book, this book will be the healer to the many that need it out there.

Lorne Driscoll

Email: iactd13@gmail.com

Appendix and Suggested Reading

Just so there are no quarrels over the definition of the words I use in this book. I am going to give the definition of one word that I got from two dictionaries, which I came across in my time. I choose to source the definition of one word only, as that one word says it all.

The Collins English Dictionary (This Edition, printed in 2006 for Bookmart Ltd)

Rape. *v* force to submit to sexual intercourse – *n* act of raping; any violation or abuse **rapist** *n*

The Reader's Digest-Oxford-Complete Word finder, A Unique and Powerful Combination of Dictionary and Thesaurus-Published by The Reader's Digest Association Limited 1990-1993.

Rape. *noun* 1a the act if forcing a woman to have sexual intercourse against her will. b. forcible sodomy. 2. Violent assault, forcible interference, violation. 3. poet. carrying off (esp. of a woman) by force. 4. an instant of rape. *verb tr* 1. commit rape on (a person, usu. a woman) 2. violate, assault, pillage 3. poet. take by force. *noun* 1. ravishment, violation, sexual assault. 2. violation, pillage, depredation, ravagement, ravaging, plundering, sack, sacking, looting, ransacking, defloration, deflowering, defilement, literary despoliation, despoilment. 3. abduction, kidnapping, seizure, capture. *v.* 1 violate, ravish, sexually assault 2. violate, assault, pillage, deflower, defile, ravage, plunder, sack, loot, literary despoil 3. See ABDUCT.

Suggested Reading

Feel the Fear And Do It Anyway ® by Susan Jeffers, Ph.D., Ballantine Books 1988

We Can Say No by David Pithers and Sarah Greene, Beaver Books 1986

What's Wrong with Bottoms? By Jenny Hessell, Jenny Hessell and Mandy Nelson 1988

Encounters With Grace by Ruth Penny, Ruth Penny 2008

God's Callgirl by Carla Van Raay, Harper Collins 2006

www.ingramcontent.com/pod-product-compliance
Lightning Source LLC
Chambersburg PA
CBHW040551010526
44110CB00054B/2639